GRANDPARENTING

Understanding Today's Children

GRANDPARENTING

Understanding
Today's Children

David Elkind

SCOTT, FORESMAN AND COMPANY
Glenview, Illinois   London

Cover photo courtesy of Stock Boston.

Library of Congress Cataloging-in-Publication Data

Elkind, David
   Grandparenting : understanding today's children / David Elkind.
      p.   cm.
   ISBN 0-673-24929-8
   1. Grandparenting—United States.   I. Title.
HQ759.9.E45   1990
305.23′1—dc20   89-38388
                                                                 CIP

1 2 3 4 5 6 RRC 94 93 92 91 90 89

ISBN 0-673-24929-8

Scott, Foresman professional books are available for bulk sales at quantity discounts. For information, please contact Marketing Manager, Professional Books Group, Scott, Foresman and Company, 1900 East Lake Avenue, Glenview, IL 60025.

To John and Ada Boyer,
good friends, wonderful neighbors,
and magnificent grandparents

CONTENTS

INTRODUCTION

"Grandpa, will you ever stop loving me?" a four-year-old girl perched on her grandfather's knee asked in a troubled voice. "Sweetheart, of course I won't. Where in the world did you get that idea?" said the grandfather. With a relieved sigh, the granddaughter replied, "Well, Daddy stopped loving Mommy, and they got divorced, so I just wondered if you would stop loving me."

Children today are growing up in a world far different from the one grandparents knew in their childhoods. In many ways it is a far more exciting, engaging world. Computers, jet travel, and microwave ovens are just a few of the miracles of the current age. But there is a downside. The deterioration of the environment, the prevalence of crime and drugs, and the high divorce rates are also very much part of our modern world. Grandchildren are the heirs of both the positives and the negatives. And thanks to changing family styles and the lack of support for children within the larger society, today's grandparents are often required to play different roles than they were expected to play in the past. You have to be part grandparent, part parent, part counselor, part confidant, and much more.

In this book I want to provide some basic information about child development and about the unique stresses of growing up in the modern world—information that may be useful as you try to fill the special roles of grandparenting that our present times have thrust upon you. I will highlight how knowing about child and adolescent growth and development is useful in understanding the way young people act and also in appreciating each of the stages in their lives. I also want grandparents to understand how stress in the home and in society affects you and how you might help offer your grandchildren the love and support they need to become healthy, happy adults.

Much of what is presented in the following pages will be familiar, simply confirming life experiences that we have all shared. Other information may be new and will provide insights drawn from research into how children develop in many parts of the world. This information can help you be better grandparents to your grandchildren when you are with them briefly or for extended periods of time. You also can use the information to help be better parents to your adult children struggling with the complexities of parenthood today.

We are living in new and rapidly changing times. Families are smaller, and grandparents live longer than ever before. These two facts alone mean that in today's world grandparents play a larger role in the lives of their grandchildren than ever before in history. And your grandchildren also need you more than was ever true for grandchildren in the past.

It is an exciting and challenging opportunity. Armed with an understanding of human growth and development and with a knowledge of the stresses that challenge that growth, you can do much to ensure that your grandchildren realize their full potential. In so doing, you also can realize your own potential— how much you have to give to the young and how much you can grow in the giving.

ACKNOWLEDGMENTS

A. Jean Lesher, the Executive Editor for books on aging at Scott, Foresman and Company, invited me to write this book about a year ago. I want to thank her for that invitation and for her gentle guidance and editing from draft to final version.

CHAPTER 1

The World of Children and Adolescents

"God doesn't have birthdays and Jesus does," a four-year-old girl told me during our discussion of holidays. It is a type of observation often made by young children and is at once quite simple and quite profound. It would, however, be a mistake to attribute to the four-year-old an understanding of the weighty theological issues raised by her remark. Simply put, young children are verbally precocious, and their language often makes them appear much brighter than they are. In early adolescence, by contrast, mental growth is in advance of verbal ability, and young teenagers often appear deceptively thick-headed. A young teenage boy may appear tongue-tied and perhaps mentally backward only because his thoughts outrace his ability to express them.

In caring for young people, therefore, we have to be alert to the fact that some of our usual clues to intelligence and personality are often misleading. With young children language facility does not signify superior intelligence any more than in teenagers linguistic clumsiness signifies inferior mental status. One of the advantages of knowing a little about the growth and development of children is that it keeps us from becoming either overly optimistic or overly pessimistic about their intellectual potential. Children and teenagers are never quite so bright nor so dull as their language makes them out to be.

A knowledge of child development does much more than give us a sharper reading of mental ability. Children quite literally see the world differently than we do. And sometimes, when we do not appreciate this, we are apt to attribute bad motives to actions that arise out of intellectual immaturity. A young child, for example, may be unwilling to share his or her toy, which we might interpret as selfishness. For the young child, however, a toy is part of his or her yet-fragile identity—part of "me" and "mine." We can understand the child's concern if we think about how we feel on having to share or part with a treasured possession. Our problem is that, from an adult point of view, a toy hardly appears to be a treasured possession on a par with something special of our own.

There is still another value to be gained from learning more about child development. We were all once children ourselves, and we have all gone through the stages that will be described in this book. We all carry forward into adulthood what we were as children. Knowing how children grow and develop can teach us something about ourselves and others. Learning about ourselves and others only stops when we allow it to, and a reexamination of our childhood, armed with new knowledge of how events in childhood sculpt later life, can give us fresh insights into our adult personality and character.

In the pages that follow, we will look briefly at some of the child characteristics at each stage of development that sometimes provide misleading cues to intelligence and personality. We will also look at what these characteristics imply for adult personality and behavior.

✧ INFANCY ✧

It may seem that the most physically able babies are likely to be the brightest, but this turns out not always to be the case. In fact, cross-cultural studies suggest that the opposite is true. Children from some cultures crawl and walk substantially earlier than children from other cultures. When these children are later compared on measures of intellectual ability, however, the children who matured more slowly do better than the children who crawled and walked early. In any given culture, of course, there are wide individual differences in rate of motor maturity that probably do not relate to later intellectual ability.

In fact, it is very difficult to assess an infant's mental ability. Even infant intelligence tests are not reliable predictors of later mental prowess. This is easy to understand. Most measures of intelligence at later age levels involve language, and that is an ability infants have yet to develop.

If infants give us few cues to their intelligence, they do provide us with solid evidence as to their temperament. According to psychiatrists Stella Chess and Alexander Thomas, there are three major temperament types that we can identify in newborns and that may persist through childhood and beyond. They call these three types *the easy child, the difficult child,* and *the slow-to-warm-up child.* As we might expect, as an infant, *the easy child* acquires regular sleeping and feeding patterns within a few weeks and has a positive approach to new situations and people. In contrast, *the difficult child* in infancy is irregular in his or her sleeping and eating patterns for months and is troubled by new people and situations. Infants of *the slow-to-warm-up* temperament eventually adapt to the home routine and to new people and situations, but they take weeks or months longer than the easy child.

At the beginning of infancy, these patterns are independent of parental personality and temperament, but within a few weeks after birth, the parents' personalities begin to interact with the infant's temperament in both positive and negative ways. A very high-strung parent can begin to make even the easy child a bit anxious and tentative. Contrariwise, a calm, easygoing, good-humored parent can have a very beneficial effect on the difficult child. The effects can also work in the opposite direction. An easygoing parent confronted with the difficult child may become anxious and upset and blame herself or himself for the problem. On the other hand, the easy child may have a settling effect on an overly anxious and worried parent.

These observations on the interactions between infant and parent temperament types also illustrate how simple it is for us to misinterpret the easily identified temperamental differences. If, say, the difficult child produces an anxious, frightened parent, we might easily read this interaction the wrong way. We expect such interactions to go only one way and therefore immediately attribute the child's behavior to the parent's personality rather than the reverse. In the same way, we are likely to attribute the easy child to the parent's facile and seemingly effortless caretaking. We need to remember, however, that infants can be as responsible for the parent's behavior as the reverse.

As grandparents, we can reassure our children when they have a difficult or slow-to-warm-up child that it is the child's temperament and not something they have done that accounts for the infant's behavior. When parents are reassured in this way, they can be a little more relaxed and less demanding of the child and of themselves, and this is really what both parent and child need most.

Although it is less common than at older age levels, we can also attribute to infants motives and intentions that are well beyond their capacities. An extreme example of such a mistake is provided by the case of a teenage mother who abused her infant son. After finally admitting that she had in fact struck her baby several times, she explained her behavior this way: "It was a wicked bad day at the store, with customers complaining about the lines and the prices while the manager was on me all day for being so slow. When I got home with a humongous headache, the baby kept crying and wailing. I told him to stop, but he just looked me in the eyes and kept on crying. He was doing it to get back at me, and so I hit him."

Fortunately, most parents are able to recognize that infants are really not capable of such motives. And while most parents will at one time or another get so frustrated and angry that they are tempted to lash out at the child, they recognize the impulse for what it is and do not act upon it.

What can infants teach us about ourselves and other adults? Long ago, Viennese physician and psychoanalyst Sigmund Freud suggested one of the reasons adults find children charming and cater to their needs. Freud argued that as we grow up, we have to give up infantile helplessness and dependency needs. But we never give these needs up entirely, and at an unconscious level we continue to harbor wishes to be helpless and taken care of. According to Freud, when we cater to the helplessness and dependency of infants and young children, we also satisfy, in a vicarious way, our own similar needs.

There is nothing wrong with that. We are all human, and helplessness and dependency are part of our humanity as adults as well as children. It is only when these infantile needs persist in too strong a way that they can cause trouble for us as adults. A case in point are men and women whose helplessness and dependency needs were never fully met when they were children. Such individuals may encounter problems if and when they become parents. They may experience jealousy and resentment of their child because he or she is getting the love and attention they desire exclusively for themselves.

Fortunately, most of us find children attractive and appealing, and this tells us that we have come to terms with our own helplessness and dependency needs and are able to accept and value them in children.

✧ EARLY CHILDHOOD ✧

Young children often give us clues to their intelligence that as I suggested earlier, may be misleading. Memory is a case in point. In some respects young children have much better memories than adults. After you read a story to a child several times, the young child knows it by heart and complains loudly if you leave out even an *a* or a *the*. Likewise, if we place ten cards with pictures of common objects on a table and then turn them over, the child is better able to remember where each picture is than we are. Young children enjoy, for a short time, a kind of photographic memory.

Like their verbal precocity, however, young children's phenomenal memory is not a good index of their mental ability. This extraordinary memory is probably a function of the fact that children have less interfering information stored in their visual memory than we adults do. As we grow older, and as our storehouse of visual memory impressions gets increasingly full, our ability to store and retrieve unaltered what we see is impaired by the clutter of all our previous visual impressions.

The clues young children give us to their personality can be as misleading as those to their memory. A preschooler is unable to take another person's point of view when it is different from his or her own. When my youngest son was four, he had a toothache, and when I asked if it hurt very much, he replied, "Oh, yes. Can't you feel it?" He could not appreciate that I could not feel what he felt. This is why a young child will sometimes be cruel to a pet. He or she has trouble understanding that the animal can feel pain. (Nonetheless, some young children seem to be able to sense this even when they cannot understand it.)

It is easy for adults to misinterpret the young child's inability to take the other person's point of view as a kind of insensitivity rather than intellectual immaturity. When we are tired and tell the young child to leave us alone for a bit and the child continues to pester us for a game or a story, it is easy to read these demands as insensitivity and willfulness. But because the young child does not feel tired, it is hard for him or her to appreciate that anyone else is. Of course, we need to keep telling the child that we are tired and need more time. But we should not take the next step and attribute the child's insistence to a permanent and negative character trait.

What can young children teach us about ourselves? The inability to take the other person's point of view is called *egocentrism*. The egocentrism of the young child gives us a fresh perspective on our own bouts of self-centeredness. As we mature, we become increasingly able to take another person's point of view even when it is quite different from our own. Nonetheless, sometimes we fall back to the egocentric mode.

This happens when we are ill or when we have had a serious failure or a spectacular success. At such times it is hard for us to appreciate the needs and feelings of others because we are so caught up in our own. Nonetheless, our situation is different from the young child's. We are capable, as they are not, of taking the other person's perspective. If we don't, it is for emotional rather than for intellectual reasons.

✧ CHILDHOOD ✧

As children move into childhood proper, the ages of six through ten, we come increasingly to assess their intellectual prowess by their progress in school, particularly by their school grades. But school grades can also be misleading guides to children's intellectual and artistic potential. For example, John Reed, the dynamic chairman of Citicorp, as a boy had trouble reading and got consistently bad grades in school. Like Nelson Rockefeller, who had a similar school history, Reed discovered as an adult that he had dyslexia, a brain-related visual perceptual disorder unrelated to intelligence.

Such examples, in which poor school performance masks true intellectual power, can easily be multiplied. Einstein and Edison were but two of the many persons of eminence who showed little promise in school. Unfortunately, schools remain inhospitable to children with an independent, original turn of mind. As our schools become increasingly test-driven, the pressure is for uniformity and conformity. Children who are eager to discover and invent often have their creativity blocked by schools that insist that they only memorize information and follow instructions. Fortunately, many creative children have the personal drive and motivation to realize their powers despite the stultifying experience of schooling.

School performance in childhood, then, is not always a valid index of the pupil's true intellectual and creative potential. In the same way, a child's behavior during this period may not always give us an accurate portrayal of his or her character. This is true because during the elementary school years, children are guided by what I have called *assumptive realities*. With the new mental abilities that emerge around the age of six or seven, children are able to form hypotheses about the ways things work and about causes and effects. As yet, however, they lack the ability to check these hypotheses against reality and therefore often give their hypotheses more credence than they give the facts.

A few examples may help make this involvement with assumptive realities a little more concrete. When we moved to Boston, our middle son was ten. He at last had a room of his own and was putting his things away when he shouted out for everyone to hear, "Someone stole my sweater," a well-worn favorite. His mother promptly explained that he would find it in the bottom drawer of his dresser. After a few moments of silence, he cried out again, "I guess whoever stole my sweater put it back." Rather than change his assumptive reality to fit the facts, he did the reverse and made the facts fit his assumptive reality.

Assumptive realities are often perceived as lies. Caught in an awkward situation, a child may make up a story that then becomes an assumptive reality that the young person feels he or she must defend. Like the young child who sees a toy as part of his or her "me" or "mine," the school-age child sees the assumptive reality as a personal creation that cannot be given up without a struggle. It is not necessarily that the young person believes the made-up story but only that it is his or her story. For the child, sticking to a false story is much more a matter of defending pride than it is of championing truth. It is well to remember that lying has a different meaning for children than it does for adults.

When our grandchildren present us with stories we know are fabricated, there are several possible approaches we can take. One is to confront the child directly with the truth. Another is simply to go along with the story rather than create a quarrel. A third approach is often the most effective. We can tell the child that the story may well be true—it does not seem that way to us, but we could be wrong. How might we go about finding out who is right? In this way we get away from personalities and make the disagreement an objective problem. We also teach children an effective strategy for dealing with conflicts about the truth.

Children also don't like to be wrong. They have what I call *cognitive conceit,* a sort of implicit belief in their own mental powers that underlies their critical approach to things like magic and their casual assertion of competence. As one young man of eight told me, "I've already had nuclear fission." It is easy to misread the child's commitment to assumptive realities and cognitive conceit as intellectual precocity and emotional maturity.

A child may tell us, for example, that he or she is not bothered about being left home alone when in fact the child may be—as a good deal of research indicates—terrified. Likewise, children will deny the unpleasant realities of their everyday lives and replace them with less traumatic assumptive realities. A child with a frequently drunk, abusive father may describe the father as hardworking and caring. While the child believes this portrayal at one level, at another he or she is careful to keep out of the father's way when the father has been drinking. We have to be alert to the fact that children's assertions of intellectual or emotional competence may conceal underlying feelings of fear and inadequacy.

Assumptive realities and cognitive conceit are not unknown among adults. Again, however, when these appear in grown persons, they have a different significance than when they appear in children. This is true because adults have the mental skills necessary to test their assumptive realities in a systematic way, whereas children do not. In adults this often results in dramatic reversals in their assumptive realities, which we rarely, if ever, observe in children. Some individuals are, for example, very much given to assumptive realities. When first meeting someone to whom they feel a liking, they may see that person as perfect in every way, and there is not enough they can do for the individual. Subsequently, as inevitably happens, when they discover a weakness, they do a complete reversal and then can find no good where before they could find no bad.

In such situations the person who is the object of the creator of the assumptive realities, and who has remained more or less constant, is bewildered by the dramatic change in treatment because it seems unrelated to anything that he or she has or has not done. Of course, this is true. The changes have all occurred in the creator's head, not in the behavior of the person who is the object of the assumptive realities. Children, in contrast, do not make such radical switches because they lack the adult capacity to test their assumptive realities. A child with a drunken father will believe the father is a hardworking and caring parent at least until he or she turns adolescent.

✦ ADOLESCENCE ✦

As young people progress through puberty, they become adult in mind as well as in body. The transition to an adult mind, like the transition to an adult body, can be difficult. Living with an adult mind takes as much getting used to as does living in a adult body. With adolescence, young people attain the ability to entertain many different ideas at the same time. When asked a simple question, for example, they can think of many different possible answers. They can give a simple factual response; a fanciful answer; a derisive, disdainful response; or a falsehood. Choosing among these possibilities is not always easy, which explains why young teenagers often seem indecisive and halting.

Again we have to be careful not to misinterpret the young person's difficulty with decision making as evidence of mental slowness. In fact, it is just the opposite. Young people often appear dull because they are so bright. They can think of so many possibilities, so many questions to ask, so many answers to give, but lack the experience that would enable them to make the most appropriate choice. With experience they will learn to prioritize their questions and answers and to respond in socially appropriate ways.

Adolescents can also give us misleading cues to their personalities and characters. For example, many teenagers often appear somewhat hypocritical. They may espouse the most idealistic values and concerns yet do little in any practical way to put your money where your mouth is, as we used to say. After a heated attack on adults for not doing anything about the people starving in Biafra, a teenager of my acquaintance spent his whole week's wages on rock music. He saw no relation between his words and a possible course of action such as donating the money to a food program for Biafran children.

It is important to realize, however, that this is only what might be called *pseudohypocrisy*. Teenagers are still at the stage where they believe that voicing or expressing an ideal is tantamount to working for and realizing that ideal. They have yet to learn the difficult lesson that there is an enormous difference between our ability to express an ideal and our ability to realize it. And it is because young people do not fully appreciate this discrepancy that they see adults as hypocritical. Only as they gain more experience do young people come to appreciate the difference between the escalator ease of giving voice to an ideal and the Mount Everest effort, self-sacrifice, and struggle needed to work toward attaining that goal.

The pseudohypocrisy of adolescents is not unknown among adults. One thinks immediately of those adults who are always quick to give voice to the cause of the poor and disenfranchised. Yet these are the same people who become incensed at how much of our taxes go to help these very same groups.

Understanding more about child development can, then, enable us to make more accurate assessments of children's abilities and personalities and thus be more supportive of children when they are in our care. We can become better grandparents and better friends. This understanding also provides some useful insights about ourselves, our adult children, and others.

CHAPTER 2

Child Rearing Today and Yesterday

Some things do not change. Children and adolescents are the young of the species and like the young of all species, show certain characteristics that are independent of time and place. For example, all infants are more or less helpless and would not survive if not cared for by adults. Your children learn best from manipulative activities, example, and restraint, and least from logical explanations. Children of school age acquire information most readily when the unfamiliar is made familiar to them through hands-on activities, discussion, exploration, and excursions. Adolescents profit most from being introduced to abstractions—like discovering that *Gulliver's Travels* is not only a story but also a political allegory—that render the familiar unfamiliar. They are challenged by the grand ideas of philosophy, history, and the arts. Philosophy, history, and the arts each place familiar experiences and events in new contexts and thus make them less familiar.

✧ PARENT-CHILD CONSTANTS ✧

These characteristics of childhood development are constants for children across the ages and are paralleled by similar verities for parent-child and child-child relations. Many of these are highlighted in literary classics. In the Bible, the story of Cain and Abel is a tragic tale of sibling rivalry. Moses grows to manhood as an adopted child of a single parent. And the timeless story of Abraham is one in which a parent is torn between competing loyalties—toward his child Isaac and his God—a kind of prophetic insight for the competing loyalties of many contemporary parents and grandparents when there is an interfaith marriage or divorce and remarriage.

In *King Lear*, Shakespeare provides one version of the age-old tragedy of misguided loyalty and affection between parent and child. In *Hamlet*, another basic family theme, revenge for harm done a family member, is tragically portrayed. Likewise, in the writings of Jane Austen, we again fine universal parent-child themes. In *Pride and Prejudice* there is the anxiety of a mother regarding the marriage of her daughters, and the two eldest daughters provide a sympathetic example of all children who have ever been embarrassed by the "unaware" comments and complaints of their parents. Marcel Proust in *Remembrance of Things Past* gives us, among so many other things, an excruciating account of one child's love and dependence upon his mother.

These themes—sibling conflict, loyalty, revenge, anxiety, pride, prejudice, embarrassment, greed, love, ungratefulness, and commitment—are part of the human family drama wherever and whenever it exists. They are embedded in our literature, in our music, in our religion, and in our language because they are timeless and universal human emotions and conflicts. So, too, are the rituals surrounding major points of passage such as birth, puberty, marriage, and death. These themes and rituals are among the many constants of family life into which all children are initiated and to which all children must adapt.

Human passions and family rituals, however, are only the constraints or limits within which individual and family lives unfold. The unique character of that unfolding is given its finished form by the culture and historical time and place in which a family lives and into which any given individual is born. As grandparents, we must review these cultural and historical circumstances to put our own position in perspective. We sometimes feel as though some of the challenges we encounter with our children and grandchildren are unique to our times and to ourselves. A glance at other cultures and at history helps us appreciate that our own personal challenges are rarely unique.

We need to look first at how culture and then historical period affects family life and child rearing. The separation of history and culture is artificial at best and is made here only for purposes of presentation. Both discussions will provide the framework for the description of families and child rearing in the contemporary United States in the last section of this chapter.

✧ CULTURE ✧

Cultures differ across both time and space. As an example of how cultures change across time, imagine what Tom Sawyer would be like if he were growing up today. His hero would probably be a jet pilot or an astronaut rather than the pilot of the riverboat *Missouri*. He would undoubtedly get around on a ten-speed bike rather than on a horse or raft and would wear jeans rather than overalls. He might well whistle and whittle less and listen to his stereo and watch television more. At school he would be introduced to computers, and at home, Aunt Polly would prepare quick meals in the microwave. Tom Sawyer was a product of his cultural times as well as of his parentage.

Homogeneous Cultures

The Tom Sawyer illustration makes another point. We are essentially a story-loving, storytelling, and story-creating species. Our lives are stories or a series of stories in which the basic human passions and rituals are played out in original ways that make each life and each family unique. It is not possible to examine cultural variations in depth, but a brief look at some of the stories different cultures tell about the basic passion of pride in their patterns of child rearing and education will illustrate how different cultures can uniquely embellish a basic human plot.

In ancient China, for wealthy families, parental pride took the form of binding a young girl's feet so that as an adult she was effectively crippled. Only families of wealth did this to their daughters. It was, in effect, a status symbol, a clear indication that the family had sufficient means that the daughters did not need to be able to work. In many American Indian tribes, parental pride took the opposite direction. Children with any physical defect or disability were often abandoned to the elements. In these societies a physical defect was regarded as a symbol of the disfavor of the gods. Even today, it is difficult to get Indian children to wear glasses or hearing aids, clearly visible signs of a "defect."

In Japan pride takes on a somewhat different aspect. From an early age, Japanese children are trained to obey and respect adults and to identify with social groups, including their family, school class, and country. Individualism is regarded as egoism and is ignored or rebuked—"The nail that sticks out gets hammered down." Pride of person in Japan becomes pride of family and of society. This works both ways. Both individual achievements and individual failures reflect upon the family and the society. That is why, in Japan, suicide is almost always a reaction to social disgrace rather than to personal depression.

In the United States, pride is quite the opposite of what it is in Japan. In the U.S., pride is highly personalized and reflects the individualism of the larger society. Children are told to take pride in their work. Their work thus reflects upon them, their effort, their ability, and their talent. When American children succeed and when they fail, they alone are held responsible. Even in our cooperative endeavors, such as playing cooperatively on a baseball team, individual members are still singled out for special attention. In America even team players are held individually accountable.

Pride takes on still another dress in French-speaking cultures. In some ways French culture is a cross between that of the Japanese and that of Americans. The French take a great deal of group pride in their language and in their culture, both of which they regard as superior to any other. An affront to the language or to the culture is taken personally. That is why if you don't speak French well, the French are likely to discourage you from speaking it at all. On the other hand, French children are very restricted as to playmates. Family and friends, rather than school class and community as in Japan, are the French child's major allegiances. Nonetheless, French children are trained to take individual responsibility for their achievements and failures. From an early age, French children are impressed with pride in language and pride of country but also with pride in self.

These few examples of how different cultures handle one of the human passions illustrate only a small sample of the possible variations of its expression. Moreover, this is but one of the many human passions that is culturally shaped. These examples can help us appreciate the enormous impact that culture has upon the ways in which we come to experience, know, and interpret our world.

Heterogeneous Cultures

The United States is clearly the most heterogeneous culture in the world, but it has never quite become the "melting pot" that it was once said to be. Many Americans retain their ethnic identity while at the same time they take great pride in their American citizenship. The cultural diversity to be found in this country as a consequence is truly extraordinary.

For example, in Brownsville, Texas, the population is 95 percent Hispanic, and the prevailing language is Spanish. In Brownsville, parents face the difficult questions of acculturation and bilingual education. At the northern extremity of the continental United States, in Bimidji, Minnesota, the population is largely American Indian, and Indian parents and grandparents have to confront the problems of widespread alcoholism and school failure among Indian youth. In the heart of Boston, a Chinese American community carries on its traditions and unique life-style. Although the Chinese community is located in the so-called combat zone of sleaze and drugs, it has the lowest juvenile delinquency rate of any ethnic group in the community. Chinese American parents and grandparents have found ways to insulate their children from many of the negative influences of the surrounding environment.

In Groton, Connecticut, a submarine base, kindergartens will often have children speaking twenty-six different languages. Most of the parents are Navy men and the women they have married in the course of their travels. These parents have to deal with the issues of constant relocation, new schools, new friends, and new languages. In Old Lyme, Connecticut, only a few miles away, the community is extraordinarily homogeneous, and there is almost no ethnic diversity and very little social mobility. Parents in this community are most concerned about local school and community issues to which the Groton parents cannot really relate.

One of the special problems this ethnic diversity poses for all parents and grandparents is intermarriage. In homogeneous cultures, interfaith and interracial marriage is rarely if ever a problem—there is little or no opportunity for it to occur. But in a heterogeneous culture, interfaith and interracial marriages are almost the norm. Parents and grandparents in the United States, therefore, are frequently confronted with the fact that their children and grandchildren may date and marry a person of a different ethnic, racial, or religious background from their own.

How parents and grandparents handle this issue depends upon their commitment to their religious, ethnic, or racial identity as well as the character and personality of the persons involved. Cultural diversity, like cultural homogeneity, poses its own special problems.

✧ HISTORY ✧

How our different human passions and family rituals are played out in child rearing and education depends very much upon cultural values and beliefs. But how children are viewed in any given society at any point in time will also depend on two major historical factors. One of these is the sociocultural focus of the country. The other is the accepted practices regarding education and human growth and development that are extant at that time.

Sociocultural Focus

At any given time in history, the sociocultural conditions within a society determine the direction and aims of its child rearing and education. In ancient Greece and Rome, where the preservation and enhancement of the state were the first priorities, education and child rearing of the patrician families were directed toward citizenship. Women in both cultures were treated as second-class citizens. In ancient Greece, schooling for young boys (but not for girls) was taken as a necessary given. There was a curriculum for boys and young men that included the arts and sciences and that began at the age of six or seven. In Roman times this education was modified to include more of the martial arts. In both Greek and Roman times, the aim of child rearing and education was to produce responsible men as citizens loyal to the state.

During the Middle Ages, the church rather than the state became the political and power center of societies. During this period, education became religious in its focus. Young men might still learn Latin and Greek, but now the aim was to read the Psalms rather than the poetry of Ovid. Young men were reared and educated to serve the church rather than the state. There was great reverence for established authority, and Aristotle became the source of knowledge for every subject from ethics to biology.

With the Renaissance and the progressive democratization of nations, the focus of child rearing and education shifted once again. Science came to replace established authority as the source of true knowledge, just as elected officials came to replace royalty, who governed by divine right. Now the aim of education was to prepare both boys and girls to be self-governing. The invention of the printing press contributed greatly to making education available to the masses and thus to the realization of true democracy. In addition, with the industrial revolution and the emergence of factory work and mechanization, education also began to prepare children to be literate workers.

The close connection between the sociocultural ideology of a country and its child rearing and education is perhaps most clearly demonstrated today in socialist countries such as the Soviet Union and China. In these countries the aim of education is to create individuals loyal to the Communist state and ideology. Until recently, this education has often been rigid and uncompromising. With the contemporary opening up of both the USSR and China to Western influence, education has also become more open to different social and economic philosophies. Yet this process is slow and halting as the recent crackdown on student demonstrations in China has made evident.

In general, then, sociocultural units seek to create by means of their child rearing and educational practices individuals who will be loyal to the values and ideologies of their country.

Scientific Knowledge

Throughout Western history, philosophers and educators have differed in their views of children and of child rearing and education. Although it is something of an oversimplification, the differences can be grouped within two general, opposing categories, both of which continue to have adherents in contemporary America. One of these views is what might be called the *environmental,* or *nurture,* view of the child, while the other might be called the *maturation,* or *nature* view. Both contain considerable truth, but both can also be exaggerated.

The Nurture Tradition. Although the view that children are entirely shaped by the environment has a long history, we can begin with seventeenth-century British philosopher John Locke's classic book, *Thoughts Regarding Education.* For Locke the aim of education was to produce rational men and women out of immature children. Effective education would produce self-regulated individuals of high moral character. Locke believed that the child's mind was a *tabula rasa,* a blank slate, and that education was therefore all-important. Education was the means of transforming the mind of a child to achieve a moral and responsible citizen.

The child rearing and educational practices advocated by Locke sound familiar, since they have been echoed by many contemporary writers. Locke, for example, suggested that parents be restrained in their praise for children's accomplishments and instead of using the rod for punishment, show them "a cold and neglectful countenance" in response to their failures. For Locke self-control was an all-important aim of child rearing and education, and he believed that children should begin to be taught this early. He foreshadowed a number of modern writers in suggesting that self-control be taught to infants by putting them on a regular feeding schedule and by not indulging their crying.

The Environmental Tradition in the United States. A direct and relatively modern descendant of John Locke was the American psychologist John Watson, whose doctrine of behaviorism was popular in the early decades of this century. Watson took Locke's notion of the blank slate to the limit. To Watson the child was an entirely malleable piece of clay, and he told parents they could have exactly the child they wanted if they used the right child rearing practices (*Psychological Care of Infant and Child,* New York: Norton, 1928):

> Give me a dozen healthy infants, well formed and my own special world to bring them up in, and I'll guarantee you to take any one at random and train him to become any type of specialist I might select—doctor, lawyer, artist, merchant chief and yes, even beggar and thief, regardless of his talents, penchants, tendencies, vocations, and race of his ancestors.

Although not quite so extreme as Watson, B. F. Skinner is the contemporary advocate of the behaviorist or environmental position. He has argued since the 1940s that the only way to modify human behavior is through the rewards and punishments (reinforcements) provided by the environment. He also contends that words like *will, freedom,* and *choice* are empty labels devoid of scientific value. What determines what we do and who we are is no more and no less than the patterns of reinforcement we have experienced. Some of Skinner's work has been incorporated into many contemporary parenting and educational practices in which *behavior modification* has become an accepted methodology. And such techniques can sometimes be useful, if used in moderation and combined with others.

The Nature Tradition. The second tradition in child rearing and education can be traced to the writings of the nineteenth-century French philosopher Jean Jacques Rousseau. In his classic book *Emile*, Rousseau set the tone for the developmental tradition in child rearing and education. The story of Emile itself is a little farfetched. A tutor takes a boy named Emile into the country and rears him by allowing him to learn through the consequences of his own actions and without the corrupting influences of family and society. Rousseau distrusted books, and other than *Robinson Crusoe*, Emile was given little to read. Education was a matter of learning from direct experience and discussion. A later American philosopher and educator, John Dewey, suggested that reared in this fashion, Emile as an adult, would be something of a prig! But what is really important in *Emile*, quite apart from its naive educational psychology, is what Rousseau said about children: "Nature wants children to be children before they are men. If we deliberately depart from this order we shall get premature fruits which are neither ripe nor well flavored and soon decay. We shall have youthful sages and grown up children. Childhood has ways of seeing, thinking and feeling peculiar to itself: nothing can be more foolish than to substitute our ways for them. I should as soon expect a child of ten to be five feet of height as to be possessed of judgment." (Translated by Barbara Foley. New York: E.P. Dutton, 1955, pp. 38–39).

Like the work of Locke, the writings of Rousseau are open to many interpretations. It is not unusual for parents and educators to use a seminal thinker's work to reinforce their own values and attitudes, which may, in fact, differ considerably from those of the author. Rousseau, for example, was read avidly by some parents and educators who found existing child rearing and pedagogy too restrictive. With Rousseau as their authority, some parents and educators did away with all restraints and restrictions and ended up with a disastrous permissiveness that was far from the balance between restraint and freedom that Rousseau advocated.

Within education the nature approach initiated by Rousseau was promoted by Johann Heinrich Pestalozzi in Switzerland and his student Friedrich Wilhelm August Froebel in Germany. In 1837 Froebel created the kindergarten, an educational program designed to meet the unique needs and learning abilities of young children. In the latter part of the nineteenth century and the early decades of this one, Italian physician and educator Maria Montessori furthered the work of Pestalozzi and Froebel by creating an array of hands-on curriculum materials for the education of young children.

The Nature Tradition in the United States. In this country John Dewey also attempted to design an educational program suited to the modes of thinking and learning characteristic of each stage of childhood. He was particularly concerned with connecting education to everyday life in order to give it meaning and substance. In Dewey's view education is most effective if it is "functional," that is, gives the child something he or she can use in the real world. Although Dewey was not opposed to classical studies, he felt that subjects like Greek and Latin were of value only to those who would teach these languages or do research that required a knowledge of them.

Dewey's ideas were translated, and too often mistranslated, into a system of "progressive" education that was quite popular during the earlier decades of this century but was totally abandoned by the 1950s. Some of the best practices of progressive education are still retained, however. One of these is the so-called project method. One variant of the project method is for the class to take a semester to work on a particular period of history, say the time of King Arthur, to read, write, put on plays about it, and so on. The project method is the best example of Dewey's major educational tenet, namely, that children learn best by doing.

The Nature Tradition in Psychology. Within psychology, the nature tradition was carried forward by G. Stanley Hall, president of Clark University in Worcester, Massachusetts. Hall founded not only Clark University but also the Child Study Movement, the *Journal of Genetic Psychology*, and the field of developmental psychology as we know it today. His two-volume work entitled *Adolescence* (1900) is a classic reference in the field. Hall emphasized the stages of development and the fact that children think about the world according to their developmental stage rather than according to what they have been taught.

A case in point was his study of young adolescents' ideas about sexuality. Hall found that young people had very distorted ideas about the effects of sexual activities like masturbation and about how young women became pregnant (many girls believed one became pregnant by kissing). Such distortion seems to be an inevitable product of adolescent thinking. For example, a recent study of adolescent ideas about the deadly disease AIDS revealed that a large proportion of young people had quite erroneous ideas about it, including the idea that it could be transmitted by holding hands!

The Freudian Influence on the Nature Tradition. It is not surprising that G. Stanley Hall was one of the first American psychologists to recognize and value the work of Sigmund Freud and his new discipline of psychoanalysis. Indeed, it was Hall who succeeded in bringing Freud to America in 1909 for his only visit to the United States. Whereas Rousseau and Hall were concerned about the child's ways of knowing and thinking, Freud was much more concerned with the child's ways of feeling and desiring. In Freud's view children also have their own unique sexuality, which goes through stages of development much like their ways of thinking and knowing. When these emerging sexual desires are blocked and not allowed to be expressed in any way, the dammed-up sexual energy can give rise to emotional disorders, namely, the psychoneuroses.

Freud's work thus illuminated a whole new side to child development, and like the ideas of so many other writers in the history of child psychology, his conceptions were soon distorted. At the adult level, one extreme was the so-called wild psychoanalysis, which proposed that since neuroses are the result of sexual repression, the cure for neuroses was sexual license. At the child rearing and educational level, Freud was sometimes understood as advocating permissiveness. Some parents and educators read Freud to mean that any form of repression is harmful. From this standpoint, children would avoid mental disturbance if they were allowed to grow up without limits, restrictions, or discipline.

Freud, of course, never advocated any such thing. Nowhere did he write that the repression of impulses or desires was necessarily bad or harmful. On the other hand, Freud did make it clear that too much repression could be unhealthy, but repression itself, Freud argued in his book *Civilizations and its Discontents,* is necessary if people are to live together in a civilized manner. Moreover, much of what is productive and creative in a society comes about through the *sublimation,* or redirection, of socially unacceptable desires and impulses. Freud never advocated permissiveness.

Piaget and the Nature Tradition. The most well known contemporary advocate of the nature position is the late Swiss psychologist Jean Piaget (1896–1980). Trained as a biologist and philosopher as well as a psychologist, Piaget had interests that were as much philosophical as they were psychological, or more so. He was concerned with the basic questions of epistemology, or how we come to know the world. Yet he was unhappy with the answers philosophers had given to this question. To his mind, each philosopher sat in an armchair and simply imagined how the child came to know the world. Piaget wanted to study this question experimentally, to put it to nature.

Piaget sought to answer the question of how we come to know the world by studying how children actually go about constructing their ideas of space, time, number, causality, and so on. At the beginning of his career, Piaget thought that his studies of children's thinking would take only a few years.

After these studies were completed, he planned to return to more important biological and philosophical investigations. In fact, however, Piaget spent the rest of his professional career studying the ways in which children and adolescents come to construct the world.

The results of his investigations, which have appeared in close to a hundred books and thousands of articles and book chapters, constitute the most extensive individual opus in the history of psychology in particular and, perhaps, of science in general. The full scope of Piaget's work has yet to be fully appreciated, nor has its impact been fully felt. Nonetheless, his work has already transformed the field of child development and has had enormous impact upon education. Perhaps more than anything else, Piaget's work reinforced a shift—already under way in the United States—from a Freudian concern with feelings and emotions to a Piagetian concern with the intellect.

Unfortunately, as was true of so many innovators, Piaget was misinterpreted and his ideas misused, particularly in education. This happened because Piaget's work is basically *developmental* in the sense that he insists that mental growth proceeds in a series of stages that are related to age and that cannot be hurried. The developmental point of view, however, conflicts with important components of the American value system.

Resistance to the Nature Position in the United States. In the United States today, we still retain many remnants of our frontier mentality. We still believe that if we don't like how things are working out, we can always pick up and move somewhere else. Even today there is still plenty of space in this country, and if we choose, we can move to states where the population is less than a million while the land mass is very large. This belief in the possibility of change and the readiness for change has made us much more open to innovation than any other society on earth. We experiment with innovations and often discard them before most other societies are ready to try them. To illustrate, we quickly accepted

Freud but are now moving away from his ideas as European countries, particularly France, are beginning to take his work seriously.

While there are real benefits to the American frontier mentality, there are negatives as well. One of these is the belief that you can achieve anything if you only set your mind to it and work hard enough. We hear this philosophy preached over and over again in our books, in our movies, and on our television screens. According to this philosophy, it is always "99 percent perspiration and 1 percent inspiration" that determines success in life. This is a very democratic belief system and encourages anyone, regardless of birth, race, or creed, to strive for success with a very real hope of making it. This value system has been important in making the United States the wonderful land of opportunity for all people.

This set of beliefs, however, makes it very hard for Americans to accept a developmental point of view. Such a view holds that there are limits to what children at different age levels can accomplish. When Piaget came to the United States and lectured about the stages of development that his research had uncovered, he was always asked what he came to call the American question: "Piaget, why do we have to wait until a child is six before he or she can attain these abilities and understandings? Why can't we teach them earlier?" As a people we are impatient with limits and constraints. As soon as we hear of a new record, we want to break it.

In our country the bulk of the early studies stimulated by Piaget's work aimed at training children to attain certain concepts at an earlier age than Piaget had reported. The failure of these teaching experiments did not deter the investigators. With great American ingenuity, they invented new tasks that children could perform successfully at an earlier age than Piaget's work seemed to warrant. Unfortunately, making tasks easier does not make children brighter. Although Piaget has had great impact upon contemporary psychology and education, the major tenets of his work, that intelligence develops with age and that there are limits to children's understanding, have not really been accepted.

How we see children at any point in history is thus never

merely a reflection of our extant scientific knowledge but is always colored by the sociocultural conditions of that particular era. Contemporary American society is a case in point. In the last half century there have been dramatic changes in the way that we perceive and rear children. But these alterations have more to do with sociocultural changes than with any revolutionary new breakthroughs in our knowledge of child growth and development.

✧ CHILD REARING TODAY AND TWO DECADES AGO ✧

The past is always prologue, and we need to look now at the immediate past and see how child rearing today differs from child rearing two generations ago, when you, the grandparents, were growing up. Some major changes have occurred in this relatively brief period that makes child rearing today vastly different and more stressful than it was several decades ago. Although none of the changes is absolute, they are all in the same direction.

Dual-Career Couples

There are more dual-career couples today than there were two generations ago. While dual-career couples can have an exciting, interesting, and challenging marriage, juggling commitments to career, spouse, and children is a constant stress. This is particularly true if, as not infrequently happens, the parents have to live and work in different communities for all or most of their work week.

Frequency of Divorce

Another change is the frequency of divorce. Although the divorce rates have moved consistently downward during the 1980s, it is still estimated that one out of two marriages will end in divorce. Divorce is an enormous stress for all the people involved, and its frequency is a comparatively new stress for contemporary families. It is true, of course, that until recently, the early death of one or both marital partners was also commonplace. Nonetheless, death is a different and in some ways less demanding stress than is divorce.

Move to Urban Areas

The number of families living in rural communities has also declined greatly over the last two generations. As families move to urban areas, they often lose the sense of community that is so much a part of rural life. In addition, the family becomes much less self-sufficient, not only with respect to the raising of their own food and making their own clothes but also in providing their own recreation and entertainment. As contemporary youth must find their recreation and entertainment outside the home, parents have lost control over this important influence on their children's lives.

Change in Technology

Still another change is technology and its effect upon family life. The changes over the last two generations have been truly enormous. Here we can just note what it means from a child rearing and educational perspective. Prior to many of today's technological wonders, the home was a natural learning environment for young children. There were, for example, muffin tins and pie plates, rolling pins and wooden clothes pins, and a scrub board that once served the same purpose as a washing machine. All of these implements and many more like them were natural and safe playthings for young children.

Need for New Learning Materials

Today, with dual-career families, frozen foods, microwaves, and fast-food restaurants, fewer and fewer families do much cooking or baking at home. Hence many of the implements that were once natural learning materials for young children are no longer available. As a consequence, parents today are constrained to buy materials for their children, and they may often be at a loss to know what to buy. In addition, since so few parents now engage in traditional household activities that allow them to involve children, many contemporary parents literally don't know what to do with their children. A major stress for contemporary parents is thus finding materials and activities for their children that are both challenging and interesting.

Acceptance of Drug Culture

Another major difference between the contemporary scene and that of two generations ago is the widespread acceptance of the drug culture by mainstream American families. To be sure, drugs are nothing new on the American scene. Around the turn of the century, opium was prescribed as a mild sedative for children, and in high society cocaine was well known. One of the lines in Cole Porter's still popular song "I Get a Kick Out of You," which was written in the 1920s, was "I get no kicks from cocaine." This was changed during the more conservative 1940s and 1950s to "I get no kicks from champagne." In more recent renditions, singers have gone back to the original lyrics.

Nonetheless, in the 1960s many rock groups advocated drug use and effectively introduced drugs to middle-class youth, for whom, up until that time, alcohol was the drug of choice. The use and acceptance of drugs like marijuana and cocaine by middle-class parents and youth is a change from two generations ago and poses a real stress to those parents and grandparents who feel that they must educate their children and grandchildren about the risks of drug use.

Less Support for Healthy Child Rearing

Another change from two generations ago should also be noted because it is a major source of stress for contemporary parents and grandparents. In many respects contemporary American society as a whole is less supportive of healthy child rearing than was true two generations ago. For example, the movement of mothers into the work force was not accompanied by the provision of quality, affordable child care to replace parental care. Public playgrounds around the country have either disappeared or badly deteriorated due to lack of funding. Schools, too, are in many cases overtesting children, testing them at too early an age, and becoming overly academic at the early grades. In response, a growing number of parents are putting their children in private schools or are engaging in home schooling.

The media are no longer supportive of healthy parenting either. Two generations ago there were strict unwritten standards for materials that might be seen or read by children. Many words that are commonplace in the media today would have been blipped out two generations ago. While some may regard the standards of two decades ago as overly puritanical and protective of youth, what we have today is at the other end of the continuum. Extreme violence, nudity, and explicit sexual activity are commonplace on television during the prime time hours when children are watching. Such material can be disturbing to children and requires conscientious parents to be constantly vigilant about what their children watch and read.

Finally, merchandisers and advertisers no longer see it as their responsibility to shield and protect children and youth. Rather, children and youth are today seen as lucrative markets who have to be sold with advertising techniques best suited to their needs and motivations. Rather than stressing good nutrition, television bombards children with advertisements for heavily sugared, salted, and cholesterol-rich products. Some merchandisers build upon parental anxiety and guilt by selling worthless products—such as a computer math program for six-month-olds—that promise if not to make the child a genius at least to give him or her a leg up on the competition.

Changes in Laws Regarding Children

Even the laws regarding children have changed. Two generations ago the laws regarding children and youth were designed for their protection. These laws recognized that young people not only had to be protected from others (child labor laws) but also from themselves (laws regarding parental consent). Today, however, the whole thrust of laws regarding children and youth has taken a very different direction. In recent years the law has worked toward protecting children's rights. The courts have supported children's "divorcing" their parents as well as using birth control and having abortions without parental consent. Children's rights are important, but so is their right to be recognized as young and inexperienced and in need of parental and adult protection.

Increased Role of Fathers in Child Rearing

A last change over the last two generations is more positive, and while it does not fully compensate for the changes in the negative direction, it does work toward the benefit rather than the detriment of children and youth. Over the last two decades and particularly among middle-class men, there has been an increased participation in parenting. In part this reflects the changed and softened image of males in our society. It is now acceptable in our society for men to show their feelings and to be sensitive to the needs of others. It also reflects the changed role of women. As more mothers enter the work force, men of necessity have to share more of the child care and household tasks.

The increased participation of middle-class men in child rearing helps counteract the lack of support for healthy child rearing in other parts of the society. While women still bear the brunt of child rearing, the new support of fathers and their willingness to be more than a breadwinner strengthens the family and provides a buffer against some of the societal pressures that make contemporary parenting so stressful.

In short, within contemporary American society, childhood as a stage of life with its own learning tasks, needs, and responsibilities is no longer recognized. Children today are looked upon as competent to deal with all of life's vicissitudes and therefore not in need of protection or special consideration. This makes the task of parents and grandparents who want their children to have a childhood, to enjoy its special pleasures and suffer its unique pains, very difficult. There is little social support today for what is generally regarded as healthy child rearing.

CHAPTER 3

Infancy

"You forget how small they are" is a frequent comment made by grandparents on viewing a new grandchild. Babies are small. On the average they weigh about 7 1/2 pounds and are not quite two feet long. Nonetheless, if I may be permitted a slight variation on the words of an old spiritual, "Little baby is small, but oh my!" Infants are indeed entitled to an "Oh my!" Far from living in a "booming, buzzing confusion" as psychologist William James suggested, the infant soon after birth has a number of quite serviceable and adaptive response patterns, and while not a connoisseur, can be quite discriminating about several choices in life. We need to look first at some of the talents of the newborn before describing some of the achievements made after this auspicious starting point.

✧ EARLY ABILITIES ✧

Babies have a number of reflexes that come into play soon after birth. Most noticeable and functional is, of course, the ability to suck. Although the baby quite naturally prefers the nipple, he or she will nonetheless readily suck anything that is at hand. This means one has to be careful, because the reflex is as powerful as it is omnivorous. I once offered a grape to my young son, expecting him to suck on it while I held it with my fingers. He snapped it out of my fingers so fast I thought I had sired a piranha. I then had to insert my fingers into his mouth to remove the grape to prevent his choking on it. Do not underestimate the power of the sucking reflex!

Another prominent infant reflex is the grasping response. It too has a lot of oomph. If you extend your two index fingers near the baby's hands, the child will immediately grasp them. The reflex is so strong that if you raise your hand you can lift the infant into a sitting position. Also "prewired" is the so-called startle response. If you are out of the infant's line of sight and quickly clap your hands, the infant will usually give the classic startle pattern, an abrupt movement of upper torso and legs. The startle response is sometimes used to test an infant's hearing.

From the first few days and weeks of life, babies are also able to make a number of sensory discriminations. They can distinguish the basic tastes—sweet, sour, bitter, salt—and show their good sense in preferring sweet over sour and bitter. Infants can also discriminate colors and distinguish their parents' voices and faces from those of other adults. The baby begins life by spending most of his or her time sleeping and eating. Within the first few weeks after birth, however, he or she stays awake for progressively longer periods and uses this time to explore the world.

✧ OUT-OF-HOME CARE OF NEWBORNS ✧

One of the questions I get asked most often by parents is, At what age it is "safe" or "healthy" to have children cared for by nonparents outside of the home? I must say, too, that I am asked this question by parents coming from two quite different positions. One group of parents who ask this question are working couples who want reassurance that putting their infant in out-of-home care is not going to do the infant any harm. Another group of parents, however, asks the question in hopes that I will say that all mothers should stay home to

Some writers are now suggesting that there be two different "tracks" for career women. One track would be for those women who wish to pursue careers but who also want to devote considerable time to child rearing. For these mothers it is suggested that employers need to provide flexible schedules, opportunities to work at home, and so on. These women would, however, not be on the track of regular promotion and advancement to the highest position in their firms.

Still another track would be available to those women who want to devote full time to their careers and put in the long days, the travel, and the commitment that executive positions demand. Presumably these women would have to make a choice between career and family, and their choice would be career.

While it is certainly true that some women fall within these two categories, it is far from being the whole truth. Some women in executive positions are able to manage a business and a family at the same time. It is not easy, but these women are exceptionally well organized and seem to manage quite well. It is also true, however, that many women find working for large companies too confining. In the 1980s women started up more small businesses than did men. Most often these are single-person businesses, and they are often run from the home. Nonetheless, many are quite successful, and the gross income from these women-run firms has quadrupled over the last decade.

Perhaps the only reasonable thing to say at this point is that women today have many more options than they did in the past and that more women are increasingly choosing the less conventional and role-stereotyped options. So long as quality child care is available, these options need not be in any way detrimental to the well-being of children nor to the strength of families. ✧

look after their children and that infants should never be put in out-of-home care.

As I look over the evidence, the major question seems to be not that of whether or not to put the child in out-of-home care but rather the *quality* of that care. While there are certain advantages to the mother's staying home with the infant during the first few months of life, there is no evidence that this is essential or that the baby will be permanently damaged if the mother is not available full time. What can be damaging is leaving the infant in substandard care—in an unsafe, crowded, dirty setting with untrained and inattentive adults. On the other hand, an infant who is cared for by a warm, caring, and responsible adult in a safe, pleasant, and accepting environment will do very well indeed.

We have to accept the fact that good parents come in all varieties. With respect to a mother's staying home, it is really her attitude that is more important than anything else. A mother who wishes to stay home and has the wherewithal to do so will be happier and a better parent than a mother who would like to stay home but can't. Her frustration will come across to her child. Contrariwise, a mother who would like to work but stays home out of a misplaced sense of duty may do less well as a parent than a mother who goes back to work soon after the child is born because that is what fulfills her and makes her a better mother thereby.

I should say, too, that there is a kind of implicit assumption that because a mother stays home when an infant is young, she is therefore a better mother. Not true. And this follows not just from what I have written above. Another preconception is the fact that just because a mother stays home and does not work at a job, she therefore devotes her life to the child. Many middle-class women who do not work outside the home nonetheless volunteer their time and are often out of the home as much as many career women.

The real question then is not at what age should a child be put in out-of-home care but rather what is the mother's attitude about working and staying home and what is the availability and affordability of high-quality child care.

✧ THE ROLE OF THE FATHER ✧

We have already noted that many middle-class fathers are more involved in child rearing and housekeeping than was true in the past. But can a father really substitute for a mother during the early months of life? Put somewhat differently, should paternal leave be an option as well as maternal leave? Again we have no evidence that being cared for by the mother during the first months of life is more beneficial than being

FADDISH CHILD REARING PRACTICES

When parents engage in faddish child rearing practices, they sometimes place grandparents in a difficult position. An example may help make this sort of situation a little more concrete. At a social function a grandmother took me aside and asked my opinion about something that was troubling her. It seems her son and daughter wanted their two-year-old son present at the imminent birthing of his sibling. They wanted the grandparents present as well. The father was going to videotape the whole drama. According to the daughter and son-in-law, this would "bring the family closer together" and all but eliminate sibling rivalry. Both the grandmother and the grandfather were a little troubled by the idea but also did not want to be thought squeamish or old-fashioned.

I told her that as far as I knew, there was absolutely no evidence that having siblings, particularly preschool children, present at the birthing of a sibling had any positive social benefits. All that we know about the intellectual, emotional, and social development of young children suggests that it would be a frightening experience and one, moreover, that the child could not really understand. Having the child present at a birthing might even backfire because the young child might well be angry and resentful at the parents for deliberately exposing him or her to this troubling experience.

My suggestion to the grandmother, then, was that she politely decline the invitation. At the same time, I did not encourage her to try to dissuade her daughter and son-in-law from their plan. When parents are emotionally committed to a particular course of action, they will not be moved by another's opinion. Although we may not be able to discourage our children from engaging in questionable child rearing practices, we should also not passively go along with them. A simple refusal to participate, without explanation, speaks more loudly than stringent and often useless arguments. ✧

cared for by the father. To be sure, men are bonier and their chests are less soft and yielding and their bearded skin less smooth and comforting than is true for the mother's chest and skin. But what is most important to infants is being held, caressed, and kissed in a loving, caring way, and fathers can do this as well as mothers.

As in the question of the age at which a child should be placed in out-of-home care, the issue of father care is one of attitude and quality. A father who is committed to the care of his infant is going to provide quality care for that infant. There is no evidence that I know of that suggests that an infant cared for by the father does any less well in the short or the long run than an infant cared for by the mother.

✧ LATER ACHIEVEMENTS ✧

During the first year of life, the infant makes rapid progress in height, weight, motor control, intellectual growth, and the attainment of social skills.

Physical Growth

During the first year of life, the baby triples its weight from an average of 7½ pounds at birth to an average of 22 pounds at one year. Growth in height is not so dramatic; on the average babies add six to eight inches to an initial twenty inches during the first year. At a year of age, most babies have about ten teeth.

Physical growth usually progresses from the head to the toes and from the trunk outward to arms and fingers. Children first learn to hold up their heads and then progressively to turn over, crawl, sit without support, stand with support, and eventually—toward the end of the first year—take a few tentative steps unaided. The child's control of small motor muscles also improves. From the full-fisted grasping of the first few weeks of life, the infant by the end of the first year is becoming able to bring together thumb and forefinger and hold objects like a spoon more securely.

Intellectual Growth

Infants also make important intellectual gains during the first year. Piaget demonstrated that the young infant does not yet have the notion of *object permanence*—the idea that an object, or person, continues to exist when it is no longer present to the senses.

Our ideas about objects and people are not inborn. We do not come into the world knowing about cars, televisions, and microwaves. Nor do we learn about these objects simply by looking at them and copying their images into our memories. Rather we come to know persons, places, and things through a laborious process of mental construction. When a baby looks at a rattle, listens to it, grasps it, and bites it, he or she is putting together the components that will result in the notion of an object that can be seen, listened to, and touched and that has an independent existence. Once the object is mentally constructed, however, the older baby, like the adult, forgets all the labor involved in its construction and sees the object as existing independent of his or her activity.

It is easy to demonstrate that the young infant does not yet have a concept of permanent objects. If you are playing with a two- or three-month-old baby—making faces, talking—and suddenly duck down below the crib or behind the high chair, the baby will not follow your path. Nor will he or she be upset for very long if at all. For the young baby, out of sight is literally out of mind. To react to your disappearance, the baby has to have an internal image of you, a cue that you were existent but absent. If you engage in such outlandish behavior with an older infant, say an eight- or nine-month-old, who has constructed this internal image, his or her reaction is quite different. At this age the baby may cry when you disappear. For the older baby, it is the discrepancy between the internal image and the absent real person that will make the baby cry. When we adults mourn a death, it is the same discrepancy between our internal image of a loved one and the physical absence that makes us sad.

During the first year of life, the infant is constructing many different "permanent objects." As a result, by the end of the first year, the infant already has quite a respectable inventory of real objects stored in memory. The presence of these permanent objects is reflected in several reactions characteristic of the end of the first year. For example, as the baby approaches his or her first year, the young child may display a fear of "strangers" and give evidence of separation anxiety when left with a sitter. Both reactions give evidence that the infant now has internal representations of the mother and father that allow him or her to reject nonparents and to protest their absence.

The fear of strangers may sometimes extend to grandparents who have not been around the infant enough for him or her to create an internal image. This fear is easily overcome if you spend a little time with the baby while the mother or father is present. And spending a little time with the child with the parents present is a good general rule to follow if you are baby-sitting or if the young child is visiting with you for a short or a long stay. Once you, the grandparent, appear, some parents are often eager to be off. We can make the transition smoother for ourselves and the children if we ask the parents to stay for a few moments while we become reacquainted with our grandchildren and they become reacquainted with us and our home—if we are looking after the children there.

Communication

During the first year, infants make remarkable progress in their abilities to communicate. Much of the communication between infant and care givers during the first year is non-verbal, but it is no less intricate or important than verbal communication. Not long after birth, for example, attentive parents can readily determine whether the child is crying because he or she is hungry, happy, or cranky. A most important milestone of communication, particularly between parent and infant, is the first consistent eye contact. Many parents report that they really feel their baby is another person after their baby has visually locked on to them.

Even though babies do not understand the parents' words, these words nonetheless communicate a great deal to the babies. When, for example, parents talk to the baby while feeding, changing, or bathing him or her, they contribute to the child's language and social development. First of all, it gives the baby a feeling for the sounds, rhythms, and sound patterns that make up his or her native language. Equally important, such loving talk communicates parental care and affection. And, as parents respond to the baby's expressions, coos, and cries, he or she has the sense of meaningful interaction with another person, a gratifying and rewarding experience.

It would be hard to overemphasize the importance of such interactions for the young infant. Psychoanalyst Erik Erikson argues that the first year of life is critical for the child to attain an abiding sense of trust that will outweigh his or her sense of mistrust. A care giver who is preoccupied, who feeds, changes, or bathes the infant in silence and who is emotionally distant in effect rejects the baby. Although not quite comparable, the adult analog would be to have dinner with someone who is neither speaking to, nor thinking of, you. Accordingly, when we actively engage an infant during care giving, we encourage the child's sense of trust in the world as a caring and responsive one.

When, as grandparents, we have our infant grandchildren for an evening, a weekend, or longer, there is much that we can do to foster this sense of trust. Talking, making nonsense rhymes, and telling the baby stories while giving care all contribute to the child's sense that the world is a safe and responsive place. Playing games such as peek-a-boo and This Little Piggy Went to Market with the infant and reading simple read-aloud stories to him or her provide valuable intellectual and social stimulation. There is really no need to buy commercial educational materials for children this age. For infants, parents and grandparents are the best educational materials ever invented.

✧ THE SECOND YEAR ✧

During the second year of life, infants continue to progress in motor development, intelligence, and social skills.

Physical Development

By the end of the first year, most children are beginning to walk unassisted. There is, however, considerable variation in the normal range for the appearance of walking. Some babies may begin to walk as early as ten months, and others may not attempt it until several months after their first birthday. Within these wide limits there is really no significance to whether a baby walks early or late; it is simply a reflection of the child's individual growth pattern.

Once a child is walking, he or she will want to embark upon voyages of discovery in the immediate environment. Because children are now better at grabbing and holding things as well as walking, it is important to take safety precautions to create a childproof environment. Objects that children might put into their mouths have to be kept off the floor and out of the areas where they might be exploring.

If we have stairs in our home, we need to install a gate to insure that the child does not go climbing, or falling, unaccompanied. It is at this stage that we have to be most careful of attractive nuisances. Wall sockets are a nuisance of this sort and should be capped with plastic covers so the young child does not push something into those inviting holes in the wall. And any and all containers of sprays, cleansers, and bleaches should be removed from shelves and cupboards accessible to young children. In childproofing a house for a toddler, it is better to err on the side of too much safety than too little.

Again, an example may help to make the importance of such childproofing concrete. A father was working on his car while it was parked in the driveway. He had some pink-colored brake fluid in a glass container that happened to be the same type of jar the mother used to store juice in the refrigerator. When the four-year-old son saw the pink liquid in the "juice" jar, he thought it was a fruit drink and drank it. The child died.

Other attractive nuisances include backyard swimming pools and unused refrigerators and freezers. In addition, parents have to be particularly careful when cooking, sewing, ironing, and using power tools with young children underfoot. Likewise, parents and grandparents have to be especially cautious when backing out of a garage or driveway when young children may be at play. Lest these warnings seem a bit overdone, it is well to remember that accidents are the leading cause of death and injury among young children.

On the other hand, it is important that we do provide young children with safe, intellectually challenging play materials. As I mentioned earlier, many of the materials of this kind such as rolling pins and pie and muffin tins are often not available. It is important in this day and age to provide toddlers with materials such as a set of alphabet blocks that the children can stack and arrange in various ways. Other materials that this age group finds interesting are wooden beads that can be strung, boards with spaces where geometric-shaped pieces can be fitted, and picture puzzles with only a few pieces. Such toys help encourage the child's interest in problem solving and improve his or her motor coordination.

Intellectual Development

Intellectual growth is also rapid during the second year. During these months children further elaborate their notions of the permanence of objects. By the end of the first year, babies have what might be called a *passive sense* of permanent objects to the extent that they may cry when a toy they have been playing with rolls out of sight. At the same time, however, the babies at this stage make no effort to retrieve the toy from its hiding place. One-year-old babies have an image of the absent object, but they are still unable to imagine that the movement that caused the disappearance of the object can be reversed. So one-year-olds cry at the disappearance of the object but do not yet grasp that it can be easily retrieved.

During the second year, however, the child acquires an *active sense* of permanent objects and takes measures to regain the object that has disappeared. For example, if you show a child's favorite sweet, then put it under a cup and then under a second cup, the child will lift both cups to retrace your actions and retrieve the sweet. The toddler now has a mental image not only of the object but also of the actions that caused it to disappear. These images are still linked to real action, however, and that is why the infant has to repeat our actions rather than go immediately to the second cup. Only later, when the child is able to manipulate mental images, is he or she able to take shortcuts in finding objects that have disappeared.

This new ability to seek hidden objects emerges as burning curiosity in many children during the second year. And it is this curiosity that makes it so important to childproof the living area in which a young child is spending his or her time. Looking for hidden things now becomes a wonderful game for the young child, who has not yet learned such tried and true adages as "Curiosity killed the cat" and "Let sleeping dogs lie." The child at this age loves things like a jack-in-the-box or a cuckoo clock because they cater to the young child's fascination with uncovering hidden objects.

Language

Another notable accomplishment of the second year is the child's rapid attainment of language. Most children speak their first recognizable word by the end of the first year. Some children talk before they walk and vice versa. The only thing this indicates is that young children often devote their energies to attaining one skill at a time. If they are busy learning to talk, they have no time for walking, and if they are intent on walking, they will have little inclination to expend energy on talking. As far as I have been able to determine, whether the child assigns more weight to walking or talking portends nothing whatsoever for his or her preferences or accomplishments in later life.

The child's progress in language is quite rapid. Single words are in fact *holophrases,* in which a single word stands for a whole phrase. A toddler who says "Mommy" may mean "Mommy, pick me up" or "Mommy, feed me" or "Mommy, pay attention to me." In general, the child's first words are nouns, with adjectives and verbs following later. Adverbs and pronouns do not usually appear until the age of four or five.

These parts of speech reflect more abstract conceptions and therefore must wait upon the child's mental development.

Both parents and grandparents can help the child acquire spoken language. Perhaps the most important thing parents and grandparents can do is to speak clearly and slowly and use standard English. Children model their language after that of their parents and will pick up their bad as well as good language habits. If children make mistakes in grammar or pronunciation, it is very important not to correct the child. The young child is learning a complex and difficult symbol system, and all efforts in this direction should be encouraged. If we repeatedly correct the child, we may give him or her the impression that the child is doing something wrong, just the opposite of what we want to do.

Rather, if the child says something like "Don do dat," we might say, "Yes, that's right. Don't do that." What we can and should do, then, is rephrase the child's statement for him or her and provide a model to copy without indicating that anything the child said was wrong. It is important to recognize that the child's difficulty is in articulation, not in hearing. If we try to mimic the child, he or she is likely to say, "No, don do dat, don do dat." The child can hear the words quite distinctly and is only having trouble in saying them.

We have to use the rephrasing technique with discretion, however, because if it is overused, the child might come to resent it as a kind of criticism. What we need to keep uppermost in mind about a child's language in the second year is that fluency is much more important than accuracy. It is much easier to encourage a fluent speaker to become accurate than to make an accurate speaker fluent.

Learning a Foreign Language. What about learning a foreign language? It is certainly true that the best age to learn a foreign language is the preschool period. There is some evidence that young children have a biological readiness to learn language that is lost by the time they attain school age. In addition, when a child learns a second language at this age, he or she is likely to learn it without an accent and to sound more like a native speaker than if the foreign language is learned later.

There is, however, a catch to this endorsement of teaching a foreign language to young children that grandparents whose first language is not English should recognize. The catch is motivation. As anyone knows who has ever attempted to learn a foreign language, it is hard work. You really have to be motivated to learn a foreign language. In some situations the motivation is more or less built in. This occurs when one or both parents are native speakers of a foreign language, as happens when parents immigrate to the United States or when U.S. businessmen or diplomats get appointed overseas. In this situation the child is motivated to learn both the language of his or her parents *and* the language of surrounding society.

For most children in these situations, it is best if the parents speak the native language at home and allow the child to learn the second language of the community from friends and at school. It can be confusing, particularly to young children, if the same person speaks in two different languages to them. If grandparents are native speakers in a second language, this is a great opportunity and time to expose the young child to the language. The only proviso is that the grandparents be consistent and not switch back and forth between languages. Even if the young person does not use the second language actively, he or she can understand it and can learn the active form much more easily later in life.

To illustrate, I know many college students whose grandparents spoke Spanish to them when they were young. The students, however, did not respond in Spanish but rather in English. Nonetheless, when these students take Spanish at college level, they are much more advanced than students without their background. Such students have a basic grasp of the structure, vocabulary, and grammar of the language so that they can pick it up quickly and speak it with more facility and less accent than students who did not hear it when they were young. I find that many students who retrieve their Spanish at the college level take great pride in their new ability to talk to their grandparents in Spanish.

On the other hand, if there is no real motivation to learn or speak a second language, most young children will fail to do so. That is why it is so difficult to teach foreign languages in the United States. We are such a single-language nation—except in communities such as San Diego and Miami—that children see little need to speak a foreign language. Contrast this with Europe, where travel between distances equivalent to the distances between our states brings people immediately into contact with other languages and cultures. European children learn second and third languages because it is very useful for them to do so.

A personal example may help make this point. When we took my two-year-old son to French Switzerland for a year, he quickly picked up French from playing with other children and from some neighbors who baby-sat for us. He spoke without accent and even picked up many colloquial expressions. When he burped, for example, he would giggle and say, "Cornicion a la creme" (pickles and cream). Yet on the boat coming home, when strangers who were not native French speakers talked to him in French, he replied in English. He was able to distinguish native from nonnative speakers and refused to talk to anyone who did not speak French properly. He was very French in that respect!

Introducing young children to a second language is a good idea if there are native speakers to whom he or she can listen. This will be beneficial even if the child does not actively speak the language. He or she will still gain enough about the grammar and speech sounds to make learning the language later much easier and more successful.

Autonomy

During the second year, the child also makes progress in getting a better sense of himself or herself. Erik Erikson speaks of this period as one in which the child has to attain a sense of autonomy that outweighs his or her sense of shame (a sense of public exposure of a weakness or failing) or doubt. It is during the second year of life, for example, that the child begins to gain control of bowel and bladder. In general, bowel control precedes bladder control. In the process of gaining control over these muscle groups, the child also strengthens a sense of autonomy, a sense of being in control of himself or herself and of his or her actions.

If we are supportive of the child's efforts at bowel and bladder control and accept accidents as a normal part of the learning process, we strengthen the child's sense of autonomy. On the other hand, if we become impatient or upset at the child's accidents, we can strengthen the child's sense of shame about being the object of displeasure and doubt about his or her self-control. To help the child acquire bowel and bladder control, we can put the child on a child's toilet seat soon after breakfast, the most usual time for bowel movements. We can also encourage the child by saying "Let go." An old trick for helping the child urinate is to turn on the water faucet while he or she is positioned for elimination. The sound of running water often encourages urination.

BED-WETTING

Bed-wetting is one of the commonest complaints parents have with respect to young children. The best advice for both parents and grandparents of preschoolers who continue to wet the bed is to *relax*. Animals do not soil their nests, and children will not soil their beds if they can possibly avoid it. If we think it is unpleasant to have to change a child's diapers, we have to recognize that it is even more unpleasant to try to sleep in wet, smelly bedclothes.

If we accept this fact and take a few simple precautions, like not allowing the child to drink much in the evening and ensuring that he or she visits the bathroom before going to bed, the problem will have the best chance of taking care of itself. On the other hand, if we make a big to-do about it, we teach the child that bed-wetting is a neat way to get attention and get back at parents without taking responsibility. That kind of secondary gain can even outweigh the unpleasantness of a wet bed. If this happens and the child continues to wet the bed as a power play, the parents may need to seek professional help. ✧

Bowel and bladder control are only a couple of the many ways in which children during the second year of life begin to try out their autonomy. They begin to feed themselves, though without the finesse they will acquire later. Likewise, they can begin to manipulate blocks, engage in finger painting, string beads, and complete simple board puzzles. They can also begin to enjoy large motor activities such as swinging on a swing and climbing up and coming down a small slide.

The child during the second year of life may try to show autonomy in still other ways. As children become more proficient in language, they may begin to say "no" even when they may want the preferred object or activity. This type of no is one way in which the child asserts his or her will and independence. The ambivalence in these self-assertions was illustrated by one of my sons when he was turning two. With an outstretched hand toward the desired cookie, he would say, "No, don wan it."

The Child's Will. These efforts at asserting autonomy have led some writers to speak of the "terrible twos." Many parents find this a very difficult time and experience it as a battle of wills. Indeed, child-rearing manuals from around the turn of the century gave parents explicit directions for "breaking the child's will." I find the opposite occurring today. Many contemporary working parents, feeling guilty perhaps because of having to put a child in out-of-home care, find it difficult to stand up to a young child's willfulness and put up with a lot of nonsense that is not healthy for parent or child.

When parents do not assert themselves with a young child, it makes it difficult for the grandparent to do so. I witnessed the following episode in a supermarket: A grandmother had a young child in a shopping cart, and he was throwing a tantrum. She was trying to reason with him, but he paid no heed. Clearly the child was used to having his way, and the grandmother could not undo what the parents had encouraged. In such situations the best thing to do is to pick the child up and hold him or her tightly while saying, "I love you, but I will not let you yell and scream when you are unhappy."

Tantrums are not the only difficult behavior shown by children during this period. Stubbornness is another. Young children often refuse to do what they are asked to do, again as an assertion of will and autonomy. There are a couple of techniques we can use to bypass this stubbornness. One is to concede the moment but not the action. If the child says no, the response could be, "Okay, you don't have to pick up your blocks this minute, but I do want them picked up by dinnertime." In this way we recognize the child's autonomy without relenting on a job that needs to be done. The other technique is to anticipate resistance and to allow for it: before resistance is expressed, we can say, "Okay, we are going out in fifteen minutes, so you will have to start finishing up."

Social Development

During the second year of life, children are also making considerable progress in social interactions. This social development is still largely with adults because young children do not yet play cooperatively with other children even though they may play side by side or "with" them. With adults, in contrast with the exception of conflicts over autonomy, the young child will also listen attentively when being told or read a story, respond positively to some requests, and begin to enjoy doing simple chores such as fetching things for parents. Young children like to feel useful and appreciate the opportunity to do simple tasks around the house.

✧ CARE BY GRANDPARENTS ✧

As the number of working two-parent and single-parent families increases, the need for out-of-home care for infants and young children has also grown apace. Unfortunately, quality affordable and available child care facilities have not kept up with the demand. The majority of children of working parents are cared for either by relatives or in family day care—usually women who care for a few children in their homes. The quality of these forms of care vary from the excellent to the horrendous.

An alternative to family day care that is becoming increasingly common is to have the grandparent or grandparents do the care giving. A number of adult children around the country are remodeling their homes to include an apartment that they can rent out or that can be occupied by a grandparent who is willing to provide child care in return. Whether or not grandparents want to take on this sort of responsibility at this point in their lives is an important decision.

Making the Decision

The decision is not an easy one. On the one hand, we love our grandchildren and take pleasure in being with them. On the other hand, should we give up our freedom and independence to move in with our grown children to become—not to put too fine a point on it—a live-in baby-sitter? You will not be surprised if the answer is that it depends. First of all, and most important of all, do not make this decision while you are suffused with some strong emotion. In a surge of love for a grandchild, you may make a decision that you would not make at a less emotional time. Give yourself some time to think it over when you are out of the situation both physically and emotionally.

Then try, as realistically as you can, to review the facts. How well do you really get along with your children and your grandchildren? Don't make the mistake of assuming that things will get better if you are around one another more, and more intimately. If there are problems, closer intimacy will only make them worse, not better. However, if you really get along well and enjoy being with them and vice versa, you might consider it seriously.

Making the Financial Arrangements

If you do decide that it makes sense for you and that you enjoy it more than you will regret your loss of freedom and independence, there is another important issue that has to be discussed, and that is finances. (I am not suggesting that you necessarily negotiate a salary.) It is important to make all the financial arrangements at the outset and have them all clearly on the table so that everyone understands them. Money is often a source of continual unhappiness and resentment, so it is well to get financial matters settled at the outset. Of course we, or our children, may not like to talk about money, but that is all the more reason that we should.

An Escape Clause

Finally, leave yourself an escape clause. Nothing is written in stone. It is sometimes wise not to burn all your bridges in the sense of totally giving up your apartment or condo. Tell your children you are going to try it out for six months or so, before they build the addition, to see whether it really works out the way you thought it would. Then, after the trial period, you can sit down and talk it over and decide whether you want to go on with the arrangement on a permanent basis.

At this stage in life, you are entitled to be a little selfish. Yes, your grandchildren need you and will benefit from your being there. But they will get along even if they just see you on the holidays or occasional visits. We really have to ask what is best for us because in the long run that will be best for everyone. If you move in and resent this intrusion on your time, the end result will be worse for your grandchildren and your children than if you never moved in at all. On the other hand, in the right circumstances and with the right people, it can be a wonderfully rewarding, enriching, and fulfilling life choice.

CHAPTER 4

The Preschool Years

The preschool years, the years from three to five, are very special. Gifted author Selma Freiburg quite rightly labeled them the "magic years." And they are magical from several different points of view. Growth during this period is truly wondrous. The squalling infant has become a walking, talking—and how he or she talks!—human being. This miracle is not the only one. The young child's body configuration, with the head about a fourth of total body length, makes him or her a bit top-heavy but gives the young child a charming lilting walk.

Young children are magic to be with as well. Because everything is so new to them, they are constantly enthused and enthralled by the simplest things: the rich brown and yellow of a caterpillar; the yeasty feel and give of bread dough; the starchy, grassy taste of fresh-picked corn; Daddy's scratchy beard; and Mommy's soft skin. All of these fresh sensory encounters are exciting and wondrous to the young child. For most of us, familiarity does not so much breed contempt as it fosters indifference. The young child can reawaken us to the many pleasures of our immediate sensory world.

Every parent and grandparent probably has his or her favorite age period. My impression is that the early childhood era is one that is most favored by grandparents, if not by parents. Preschool children seem to show a particular affinity for grandparents. Perhaps they sense the maturity and stability that is only partial in parents who are still trying to sort out parenting, marriage, and career roles. Because young children are experiencing so much that is new, it is reassuring and comforting to them to have adults about who are at ease with themselves and the world. With such adults, children can feel free to explore the environment. They can try out new words and initiate new activities with a sense that the world is secure and that their explorations will be understood as just that—explorations, not mischief.

✧ MOTOR DEVELOPMENT ✧

We need to look a little more closely now at the remarkable achievements of these preschool years. As the child grows in height and weight and develops greater motor control, he or she becomes capable of a whole new range of motor skills. By the age of three, the average child is more than three feet tall and weighs about twenty-eight pounds. Many children by this age can ride a tricycle, push a scooter, catch a large ball, go up and down a slide, and button and unbutton their jackets.

By age three, children have also acquired considerable dexterity with the small muscles of the hand. Now they can fill sand pails at the beach and begin to build with blocks at home or in preschool. If you place a small stool in the bathroom and have a towel hook where the child can reach it, the preschooler can also wash and dry his or her hands. At this age children have also made several steps toward dressing themselves, though they may still have trouble tying their shoelaces. (Shoes closed with adhesive snaps are now in vogue, but I still believe it is useful and rewarding for children to learn to tie their own shoelaces.)

Most children are fully toilet trained by the age of three, but some children may continue to have accidents. In general, it is best for us to accept such incidents for what they are, namely, occasional lapses on the way to full control. If we can accept them lightly, children can do likewise. Some children continue to wet the bed on a more or less regular basis. For many children this may be no more than a matter of maturation. A few simple practices, such as not allowing the child to drink much before bedtime and encouraging the child to go to the toilet just before going to bed, will often help resolve the problem. Most children will naturally stop wetting the bed if we do not make it such an issue that the child can, however unconsciously, use the practice to gain such other things as undue attention.

With all of these new motor abilities at their command, young children are eager to be of help around the house, and they should be encouraged to do so. Young children can learn to shell peas and to wash carrots and potatoes. Involving children in everyday household work where their assistance really contributes to the success of the task helps them feel important and needed. They like to do errands and such chores as taking out small bundles of trash. When we involve young children in these ways, it is very important that it not be busy work that we have created just to give them something to do. The tasks should be meaningful and really save us time and effort. Then we can, with honesty and gratefulness, thank the child for helping.

The development of motor control clearly has other social implications. Erik Erikson described the preschool years as a period during which the balance between the child's sense of *initiative* and sense of *guilt* is determined. If children are allowed to initiate activities prompted by their new motor abilities, their sense of initiative—that they can get things started on their own—is supported and enhanced. On the other hand, if we scold the child for his or her efforts to help or for taking apart discarded clocks or telephones, the child's sense of guilt—a sense of having done something wrong and of being a bad person—will be strengthened. While a bit of guilt is a healthy thing, too much is not. We need to give young children sufficient support for their explorations so that they leave this stage of development with their sense of initiative much stronger than their sense of guilt.

Young children quite literally see and think about the world differently than we do.

Purposeful Thinking

First of all, young children tend to think that everything in the world has a purpose, and they have little understanding about chance happenings or accidents. (Nonetheless, they quickly learn to say, if not to understand, "it was an accident" if they happen to break something.)

Much of the literature written for young children reflects purposeful thinking. Young children are fascinated by stories that explain how the elephant got its short tail or how the leopard got its spots. Nothing in these stories is left to chance or natural selection.

Absolutism

The literature for young children also reflects another facet of their thinking at this age level, namely, absolutism. Characters in fairy stories are either all good, like the fairy godmother or Prince Charming, or all bad, like the wicked witch or the nasty giant. This absolutism also helps explain why young children sometimes fail to recognize their parents when they are all dressed up. Having seen their parents in everyday clothes, it is hard for them to appreciate that it is the same parent in the dress-up clothes.

Animism

Young children's thinking also tends to be animistic, in the sense that they may attribute life to inanimate objects. To a young child, a stone rolling down a hill may seem to be alive because he or she equates movement with life. It is not really until middle childhood that children understand life and death in biological terms. Prior to that, death seems to be only a going away that is temporary. As one four-year-old asked after attending his grandfather's funeral, "How long do we have to wait before Grandpa isn't dead anymore?"

Coincidental Causality

Still another facet of young children's thinking might be called coincidental causality. Young children tend to believe that two events that occur together cause each other. A child who is troubled may cling to a teddy bear or blanket and find that its warmth brings comfort. The child may then come to believe that the teddy or blanket not only brings comfort but wards off troubles. It is this kind of thinking that helps explain why young children become so attached to particular "security" objects. It also explains why, when they attain a new level of thinking after the age of five or six, they are willing to give up the security of the teddy or of the blanket.

Egocentrism

A different, much misunderstood characteristic of young children's thinking is *egocentrism*. When applied to the thinking of young children, egocentrism does not mean selfishness or self-centeredness. Rather, it refers to young children's limited intellectual powers that leave them incapable of putting themselves in another person's position when it is different from their own. Many four-year-olds, for example, may know their own right and left hands. If, however, you place a four-year-old opposite yourself and ask him or her to point to your right or left hands at this stage of development most children are unable to do so correctly because they cannot mentally put themselves in your position.

It is very important not to mistake this intellectual limitation for anything more than that. For example, sometimes a child may seem cruel to a pet or insensitive to a parent's or a grandparent's indisposition. While we should call such incidents to the child's attention, we should not attribute them to bad character. Rather, we might say, "It hurts the cat when you pull its tail." Or we might say, "When you play so loudly and I have a headache, it makes my head hurt more." In this way we recognize that the child is not engaged in a particular activity out of bad motives but rather from egocentrism, which does not permit full appreciation of the impact of his or her actions upon others.

Information Processing

Another facet of young children's thinking is that they process information much more slowly than we do. A personal example may help make this point a little more concrete.

When my sons were young, I took them to see a circus that had just come to town. I had fond memories of the circuses that I had seen as a child and was eager for my sons to experience that same special excitement, awe, and wonder that circuses engender. I bought tickets for good seats and was anticipating the pleasure the boys would get from the performances. Yet I had a hard time getting them to attend to what was going on in the rings. All they seemed concerned with were the peanuts, popcorn, hot dogs, and soda that were being hawked all about us.

I said, "Look at the lady in the pink dress on the elephant!" I said, "Look at that man on the trapeze!" But their attention seemed solely upon the man in the white coat. Disappointed and unhappy, I drove home thinking that television had robbed children of the opportunity to enjoy the special pleasures of the circus. Several weeks later, to my great surprise, the boys began to talk about the circus, about the lady in the pink dress and the man on the trapeze. What I hadn't appreciated was the fact that a three-ring circus is a great deal of stimulation for a young child. They had registered much of what was going on, but they needed much more time than older children and adults to process and sort out the information.

✧ LANGUAGE ✧

"First you can't wait for them to talk, and then you can't wait for them to be still," is a not infrequent comment of parents

---

and grandparents experiencing the loquacity of the young child. Like so many other enchantments in his or her young life, language is a fresh new wonder to be savored, enjoyed, and even squandered—after all, there seems to be a limitless supply. And young children are often quite outrageous in their comments. They speak openly and unabashedly about the man with the shiny head or the woman with the skinny legs. Although they know that words can hurt—they don't like being called names—their inability to take another's point of view makes it difficult for them to appreciate that their own words can be equally harmful.

It is in their use of language that young children show their humanness. Although animals can be taught to use a sign language, it is not clear that they could ever create a sign language of their own. But as children begin to perfect their language ability, they also begin to create new phrases that reflect their special way of seeing the world—a uniquely human capacity. A few of the phrases that children have created and that I have gathered over the years are as follows:

"A furry sheet"	blanket
"Daddy's work purse"	briefcase
"Choo choo bird"	airplane
"Stocks"	Mommy's stockings, Daddy's socks

Young children are unaware of having created these phrases and use them as if they were the same as words learned from parents.

Although children's progress in language is quite rapid, children sometimes make characteristic "mistakes." A preschool child might say, for example, "My feets are cold," or "He dooed it." Such "errors" really reflect the fact that the child has learned the general rules of pluralization or of the past tense but has not learned exceptions like the plural *feet* or the past tense *did* for the verb *to do*. As in the case of articulation problems, the best strategy is simply to model the correct plural and tense forms. The child will eventually correct himself or herself as a result of listening to us, and this is the most effective mode of language learning.

Reading Instruction at an Early Age

In recent years it has become fashionable to teach young infants and young children to read, and there are many commercial programs available for this purpose. Such programs, however, fail to appreciate the complexities of the reading process and tend to identify reading with the ability to recognize and name words. But naming words is far different from true reading with comprehension. These early reading programs encourage young children to learn by rote, or by memorizing words; they have no other learning capacity with which to learn this complex material. The danger of this early emphasis on rote learning is that the child may become fixated on this learning mode and try to learn everything in the same mindless way when in school.

There is another danger to such early instruction that derives from the young child's mode of thinking. Young children tend to believe that adults are all-knowing and all-wise, that they are godlike creatures. Fortunately or unfortunately, when they get to be six or seven, they discover that adults may not know one specific thing and from that remarkable discovery they often conclude that adults don't know much at all! But at the preschool level, the child still believes in the adult's omniscience. When this all-wise, all-knowing adult tells the child he or she should learn something, like reading, and the child can't (for developmental rather than motivational or intellectual reasons), what does the child do? He or she does not blame the omniscient adult. Rather the child blames himself or herself and says, "I must be dumb." This self-evaluation can become a self-fulfilling prophecy in the sense that the child then takes any failure as his or her due and any success as an accident.

Certainly, if a young child learns to read on his or her own—about one to three in a hundred children do so—we should support the child's achievement and provide appropriate books and allow the child to read aloud to us if he or she chooses to do so. But there is really no need to instruct a young child in reading if he or she shows no inclination in that direction. If you are a grandparent and the parents are insistent on teaching the young child to read, it is best not to argue with the parents about it. What you can do is politely refuse to participate in such teaching and continue to read to the child. This polite refusal to participate is often more effective in altering parental behavior than a lively and usually unproductive argument.

Fairy Tales and Fantasy

At meetings with parent groups, I am often asked another question about reading. Some parents and grandparents wonder about reading fairy tales to young children or stories about Santa Claus and the Easter Bunny. Their concern is that these are fantasy, a fiction, and reading this material to children amounts to not telling them the truth. Aren't we supposed to be honest with our children? And later, when children discover these are lies, won't they be angry and disenchanted with us?

Not really. Even at an early age children know at an intuitive level that Santa Claus is a fantasy. Most youngsters would be quite surprised to see a Santa Claus come down the chimney! When hearing fairy tales, children do the same thing we do when we go to a play; they suspend critical judgment and believe that what is acted on the stage is really happening. And when children get older and become more aware of what they once knew intuitively, they do not hold this exposure to fantasy against their parents at all. In fact, giving up the belief in fairy tales is an important marker of their intellectual progress. As one youngster told me proudly as he put up an Easter display on the bulletin board at his school, "I don't believe in the Easter Bunny anymore!"

✧ THE GROWTH OF KNOWLEDGE ✧

The young child also makes important progress in acquiring knowledge over and above his or her proficiency, or at least fluency, in language. By three years of age many children are beginning to arrive at elementary classifications of objects such as toys and of qualities such as red. Nonetheless, they often make mistakes that are charming. For example, a young child may call every man he or she sees "Daddy," confusing the one male daddy with the many male men.

Sometimes language masks limitations in the child's knowledge. A child may, for example, be able to count to ten without error. When, however, we ask the child to count, say, ten pennies, we see the limitations of the young child's understanding of the concept of number. Even though the child can count correctly verbally, he or she is often unable to apply this verbal knowledge to real objects. When attempting to count ten pennies, the child counts the same penny more than once and neglects to count others. Some children may even "forget" what they were asked to do in the first place and come up with a number at random as their result.

Children's Questions

One way young children increase their knowledge is through asking questions, and they are notorious askers. In responding to the questions of young children, however, it is important to remember that they think purposefully. When a young child asks, "Why does the sun shine?" he or she is not asking for an explanation of the relation of heat and light. Rather the child would readily accept a reply to the effect that the sun shines to keep us warm and to make the flowers grow.

Some parents and grandparents may object that this is the wrong way to respond to such a question. After all, the child is asking a scientific question and is entitled to the correct explanation. To respond in the manner suggested above is not only giving the child wrong information but is also talking down to them and underestimating their intelligence. While such objections are understandable, they reflect the adult rather than the child point of view.

First of all, when we answer a question at the child's level of understanding, we communicate that we do know what he or she is asking. This is very reassuring to the child and encourages further question asking. On the other hand, if we responded to the question about the sun with, "Heat makes light," the child would ask why, and that would entail an explanation far more complex than what the child could grasp. In the end, all the child would learn from such an answer is not to ask any more questions. Nor are we misleading the child. The sun does keep us warm and does help plants grow. Whether it was designed for this purpose is another matter, but the answer is certainly correct as far as it goes.

Another issue in dealing with children's questions arises when these questions deal with such delicate matters as sex. Whenever this happens, it is always wise to ask the child what he or she thinks before we venture a reply. In asking questions, children's verbal ability may again mask their limited understanding. For example, one young child happened to watch a TV program dealing with AIDS prevention. He then asked his mother, "How do you prevent AIDS?" Fortunately, the mother thought to ask the child what he meant before she launched into a detailed discussion of the subject. She said, "What do you think?" To which he replied, "Don't have intersections and buy condominiums!" Children try to make sense out of the world as best they can, and this effort may result in an understanding far removed from what is the adult meaning. Children are always more than happy to give us an answer to the question they are asking.

✧ SOCIALIZATION ✧

There is also remarkable progress in socialization, in the acquisition of skills for dealing with other people, during the early childhood period. Infants will occasionally respond to one another, and two-year-olds will often play side by side, but true cooperative play does not usually appear until about the age of four. It is at that age that young children begin to be able to take turns and share projects. It is also at about the age of four that children begin to talk about "my friend." Adults are still seen as all-powerful, all-wise, and all-knowing and tend to be obeyed without much resistance. The exception occurs when the young child sees a demand or request as impinging on his or her sense of pride or dignity. I knew one young man who refused to go to his room as punishment for making a mess. It offended his dignity to be punished, since he "did not do wrong things."

Frames

An important aspect of socialization is the notion of the frame, a repetitive social situation with its own rules, expectancies, and emotional patterns. Frames would include such familiar social routines as having a meal at a restaurant, waiting in line for any number of different things, visiting relatives, and a great many other familiar social routines.

The rules, understandings, and patterns implicit in waiting in line provide a concrete example of how frames operate. When we wait in line, it is understood that we maintain our position and do not push ahead and that we do not—or at least appear not to—attend to the conversation of other people nor become overly familiar with them despite the close physical proximity. The emotional undercurrent of a frame becomes apparent when someone attempts to go to the front of the line without waiting his or her turn!

A large part of the young child's socialization consists of learning a multitude of frames. Consider the dinner frame with all family members present. Among the many rules a child might be asked to learn are: Do not start until everyone has been served, Do not talk while you have food in your mouth, Ask for food to be passed—do not grab it across the table, Take only your portion and leave enough for others, and Do not leave the table without asking to be excused. Children learn these frames partly from imitating their parents, partly from direct instruction.

Understanding the dynamics of frames is useful in dealing with young children. Consider the case of frame switches. A child is busy playing with his or her toys, and the parent needs to go out shopping and wants the child to get ready to go out. This requires the child to make a frame switch. The child must switch from a playing frame to a going shopping frame. It is always hard to switch frames, and this is particularly true for the young child. Even if the child enjoys going shopping, he or she may resist because of an unwillingness to switch frames rather than because of a reluctance to go shopping.

Once we recognize that we are going to require a frame switch, we can ease the child into it by preparing him or her in advance. A half hour before you are ready to go, you can say, "We are going shopping in about half an hour, so you should finish up your project and start putting things away." A little later you can say, "Fifteen minutes to shopping lift-off. Better get your things put away." By announcing the frame switch in advance and at several different times, the child is much better prepared for it and will make the switch much more easily than if he or she is abruptly told, "Okay, let's go."

Frame Clashes. Not infrequently there are also what might be called child-to-adult frame clashes. Consider a child who always forgets to put his or her toys away after playing with them. The parent or the grandparent frame is "After you use something, you put it away." But this is not the child's frame, which is most often implicitly "Play with it until you lose interest and then go on to something else." Part of our upset and unhappiness with a child with this sort of frame is that it clashes so strongly with our own.

One of our natural human reactions, when there is a frame clash, is to attribute bad motives to the other person's behavior. We sometimes do this with children as well. In the situation described above, we might attribute carelessness or sloppiness to the child's behavior. On the other hand, if we recognize that the child hasn't fully learned the using toys frame, we can restate the rules of such frames. We might say, "I'm glad you had a good time with your blocks, but you know whenever you play with them, you should put them back. Okay?" In so doing, we recognize that it is frame learning, not character, which is at issue when a child fails to put things away.

Spoiled Frames. Sometimes frames can be spoiled, and the resulting emotional reactions need to be dealt with. This happens most often with frames associated with anticipating something. Expectation of a special treat or a trip to the zoo or a night at the circus constitute an anticipatory frame. If, for whatever reason, we cannot complete an anticipatory frame, the frame is effectively spoiled. Instead of the anticipated joy and pleasure, the child has to deal with the sadness of losing what he or she had looked forward to. When we have to spoil a frame, we need to be aware how painful this is to a child. We should apologize, give our reasons for having to spoil the frame, and say that we will try not to let it happen again.

Frames, then, are a useful way of looking at and understanding the young child's behavior. Indeed our behavior is regulated much more by complex social frames than it is determined by simple habits. When we understand the dynamics of frame switches and clashes as well as of spoiled frames, we have powerful tools for effectively handling many of the socialization problems presented by young children.

Manners

At this point, it is important to say something about manners. In my experience, parents much more often than grandparents make the mistake of demanding good manners on the part of the child without feeling the need to show good manners to the child in return. The reason is that we adults tend to think that children are much more like us in their thinking and least like us in their feelings. In fact, just the reverse is true. Young children are least like us in their thoughts, most like us in their feelings. When we break a promise or unintentionally say something harsh, the young child feels exactly as we do under similar circumstances. It is very important to say "I'm sorry" to a child on such occasions. And it is equally important to say "Please" and "Thank you" to young children when we would say these words to adults. If we show good manners to children, they will learn to show good manners to us.

◇ DISCIPLINE ◇

What is the appropriate discipline for a young child? After all, young children do misbehave, get into mischief, and sometimes take dangerous risks. How do we handle misbehavior? The aim of discipline is education. We want children to learn to behave properly, not just to stop misbehaving. Looked at in this way, the question becomes, How do we best educate young children? In my opinion physical and verbal punishment are not effective methods of teaching young children. Children learn most through modeling and imitation. What children learn from physical and verbal punishment is to use these methods themselves!

There are exceptions, of course. Sometimes children need to be taught what might be called *healthy* fears—fears of dangerous objects or actions that are sometimes learned through punishment or negative consequences or both. When a young child suddenly dashes into the street and we grab him or her back and smack that well-padded bottom, we are expressing our emotions of anxiety, fear, and love. The child appreciates that reaction and will model our fear and anxiety and show caution at the curb, which is just what we want to teach the child. When we hit a well-padded child as part of our emotional protective reaction, this really does the child no harm and can help him or her learn healthy, self-protective fears.

After the age of four or five, however, physical punishment is usually not called for, especially when it is administered long after the fact of the misbehavior. After the age of six or seven, children can be reasoned with, and this is a much preferable form of discipline. Aggression begets aggression, and when we try to resolve issues with older children by means of physical punishment, we end up teaching them that physical punishment is the way to handle misbehavior. It is not really the message we want to teach.

The essence of sound discipline is not a set of techniques but rather an attitude that conveys to the child that we are in charge and that we know what we are doing. This is a difficult attitude for many parents to adopt. Even with young children, some parents feel that they are victims of the child's bad behavior and can do little to stop it or prevent it from happening in the future. Parental entreaties to stop crying or to stop having a tantrum have little if any effect. The child senses that the parent does not know how to handle the situation and takes advantage of that knowledge to garner attention and win control.

In fact, however, children don't like to be in control and would much rather that the parent took charge. When we are with someone who knows their business, we can relax. Children are the same. When they are with a parent, grandparent, or teacher who knows what he or she wants to do and how to go about doing it, they feel comforted and at ease. To exercise discipline, therefore, we have to think through what we want and communicate that clearly to the child.

For example, your granddaughter may refuse to go to sleep and continues to come into the room where you are entertaining guests. At some level she knows that you are unlikely to try to teach her a healthy fear when guests are about. Hence she takes advantage of this moratorium. At such times you also need to take charge. You can introduce her to the guests and then take her away and say, in a voice that leaves no doubt in the child's mind about your meaning, that you expect her to stay in her room for the rest of the evening—period.

A tone of conviction will do more than a dozen threats of punishment or rewards. Threats of punishment and reward suggest that we are really not in control and have to barter with the child. A tone of conviction, however, leaves the child to conjure up what punishments might be in the offing. The uncertainty will be more effective than specific threats that the child knows will probably never be translated into action. In discipline as in drama, it is always better to leave things to the imagination than to spell them out.

Another discipline issue arises when siblings fight with one another. Again, the adult must take charge by defusing the stirred-up emotions. This can be done by asking each child in turn for his or her explanation of what started the battle. This approach has several advantages. It immediately makes the conflict a verbal rather than a physical one and thus teaches children that differences can be expressed verbally as well as physically. By not playing favorites, by listening to both children carefully, and by coming to a judicious, fair decision, the parent models an effective strategy for conflict resolution.

Whenever there are discipline issues, the adult has to communicate that he or she is in charge and in control of the situation. Having a sense of being in control of the situation is the most effective discipline tool the parent has. If you, as a parent or grandparent, feel that you know how to handle the situation and communicate this to the child, the misbehavior is no longer a problem. If you communicate in your words and body language that you are at a loss as to what to do, the misbehavior will only get worse. The most effective discipline, then, is not a set of techniques but rather an attitude and a sense of being in charge. The golden rule of discipline is *Say what you mean and mean what you say.*

✧ PLAY ✧

One of the least understood features of development in early childhood is the importance of play. In young children, play is best thought of as a mode of learning. Play in young children is always a form of generalization, a fundamental learning mode. When children play house, for example, they are generalizing from their experience at home. The same is true when children play store, use puppets, or transform a block structure into a castle. Certainly imagination and creativity are at work here, but they are forms of generalization as well. The gifted artist or writer generalizes from his or her personal experience in novel, interesting, and insightful ways.

It is often said that play is the young child's work. Unfortunately, this is not the case at all. Children work as well as play, and they learn through both activities. If play is going from the particular to the general, work is the reverse. Whenever we work, we go from the general to the particular. Whether it is the artisan, the professional, or the mechanic, work is always bringing general principles to bear on a particular case. An artist sculpting, a surgeon operating, and a machinist turning a wheel on a lathe are all applying general principles to particular cases, and this constitutes work.

When children tie their shoes, use a knife and fork when eating, or hold and write with a pencil, they are moving from a general motor skill—the opposition of thumb and forefinger—to a specific application of that skill. Likewise, as children learn to say please and thank you at the appropriate times, they are going from general rules about good manners in saying please and thank you to using these terms correctly in particular instances. So young children play and young children work, and they learn from both activities.

✧ NURSERY SCHOOL AND CHILD CARE ✧

Over the last decade there has been a dramatic increase in the number of preschool children in out-of-home programs. In part this reflects the 80 percent increase in the number of mothers of children under six who are in the work force. It also represents, however, a growing appreciation of the importance of preschool education. This has meant that child care facilities have become much more concerned with the educational quality of their programs, while early-education programs have often extended their days to provide more child care.

Today, the distinction between nursery school, concerned with socialization and education, and child care, concerned primarily with looking after the children when the parents are at work, has all but disappeared. It is recognized today that there can be no education without child care and no child care without education.

As I suggested earlier, the really crucial issue in the choice of nursery school or child care facility is the *quality* of the program. Trained staff; low staff-to-child ratios; clean, attractive, well-provisioned rooms; and easily accessible play areas are all things to look for in an early childhood program. The bulk of the evidence we have today is that if children are in a quality program, even from an early age, they will benefit in many ways. Nor is there any evidence that children in quality programs are any less bonded or attached to their parents than children who have spent their early childhood years at home.

Other things being equal (namely, a positive parental attitude toward child care and a nonstressed home environment), most children in high-quality child care will do as well as they might do at home.

✧ TELEVISION ✧

How much television should children watch? That is a question I am often asked when I meet with parents. But there is another question, of equal or greater importance, that parents don't ask and that needs to be discussed first. This other question is, What is the impact of television upon the parent-child relationship?

Television and the Parent-Child Relationship

Television is particularly attractive to young children. Young children are, by and large, blocked from gaining information from books and even from the radio thanks to their limited language comprehension and their inability to read. But television bypasses these language skill deficiencies by presenting children with visual images accompanied by oral language. Thanks to television, therefore, young children have access to information they could never have received directly before. Only in the age of television could millions of young children have immediate access to the tragic shuttle disaster.

The attractiveness of television to young children has had a negative effect on parent-child relations. Some parents find television a very convenient baby-sitter. While this may do no harm when used in moderation, it is very tempting to use television to amuse children even when parents have the time to talk and play with them. When parents give in to this temptation, it limits the opportunities for meaningful parent-child interactions. Parents, however unconsciously, make their own activities more important than interaction with their children.

Unfortunately, when this happens, children may change their priorities as well. If such parents are working and are very restricted in the times they have to spend with their children, they may find that the children want to watch a program more than they want to spend time with them. In too many families, television has reduced the amount of meaningful parent-child talk and play.

There are a couple of things we can do to change this pattern. As grandparents, we can take the time to read to our grandchildren, to play games with them, and take them for walks and talk with them about what we see and hear. In this way we help make them aware of all the wonderful information available in books and the immediate world. If children wish to watch television, we can look for a quality program, watch the program with the child, and then take time to talk with the child about the program after it is over. In this way we can help our grandchildren be discriminating and reflective about what they watch on television. Television is here to stay, and what we need to do is help children be intelligent, discriminating, and selective viewers.

How Much Television Should Young Children Watch?

There are no hard-and-fast rules about how much television viewing is good or bad for children. In most cases we have to use common sense. Preschool children, for example, need to do a lot of exploring and manipulating of their immediate world to get a solid grasp of the basic concepts of that world. These concepts include colors and shapes, textures and patterns, not to mention physical relations such as up and down and behind and under. Children also need to get a good sense of physical space by walking and running. If children spend too much time in front of the television, it limits the time they have to learn about the real world.

My own feeling is that two or so hours of television watching each day is more than enough for most preschoolers.

To be sure, there are always special circumstances when a child might watch more than that. But if young children are spending more than two hours a day regularly watching television, they may well be losing out on important learning experiences. They may also be acquiring a passive attitude toward learning, which a more active involvement in their world would prevent.

It should be said too that the latest television technologies have given us much more control over young children's television viewing than was true in the past. The advent of cable television programming vastly expands our choices and makes available quality programs at all times of the day and evening. In addition, the introduction of VCRs and videotapes means that we can now provide children with quality programming and good films whenever we choose. Given these new technologies, there is really no excuse for allowing young children to watch anything that happens to come onto the screen. We can and should exercise a great deal of control over what young children watch on television.

✧ CHILD ABUSE AND OTHER DANGERS ✧

There is a great deal of concern these days about child abuse. Many parents who have their children in out-of-home settings or in nursery schools are concerned about this issue. Some parents believe that children should be taught to protect themselves against adults who might want to do them harm. Unfortunately, such teaching may end up doing more harm than it does good. There is simply no way that young children can protect themselves from an adult who would abuse them. A number of studies show that the young children do not understand the difference between "good touching" and "bad touching" or really grasp the concept of the stranger.

It is our responsibility, not the child's, to ensure that the adults to whom we entrust a child's care are responsible. Fortunately, the great majority are. Most child abuse occurs among relatives and at home rather than with strangers at child care facilities. Certainly, young children can be taught some self-protective healthy fears such as not running in the street, not touching a hot stove, and not eating things that have fallen to the floor. But defending themselves against adults who would do them harm is a far different and much more complex danger against which they can take no effective action.

In the same way, it makes little sense to alarm young children about the dangers of nuclear war, drugs, and AIDS. All such information does is tell children that there are terrible things to be frightened of without giving them any concrete way of dealing with the fear and anxiety. As a general rule, it is best not to tell children about a danger unless we can give them some concrete ways of avoiding or dealing with that threat. Otherwise all that we accomplish is to make young children anxious to no purpose. If children ask us about these matters, as I suggested earlier, the best strategy is to ask the child what the word or words mean. More often than not the child's interpretation is far more innocent than our own.

In many ways, as Dickens wrote long ago, these are the best and the worst of times. We need to make every effort to expose young children to all that is beautiful and wonderful in the world—they will learn about all that is terrible and frightening soon enough.

CHAPTER 5

Childhood

In this book "childhood" refers to the years from five to eleven or twelve. From a physical point of view, this period of development is marked by a slowing down of bodily growth and a consolidation and greater coordination of motor skills. Intellectually, children attain what the ancients called the age of reason, the period in life when children acquire the ability to reason in a syllogistic way (for example, All men are mortal; Socrates is a man; therefore Socrates is mortal). Children show their new-found reasoning powers in many different ways. School-age children demand rational explanations and are fervent in their rooting out of sham and deception. Woe be to the hapless magician confronting a group of nine-year-olds. At this age children love riddles (Why did the tomato blush? She saw the salad dressing!) that challenge their reasoning powers.

Children also make considerable progress in social development. Although they become interested in making friends at about the age of four and enjoy playing with their peers thereafter, the peer group itself does not begin to exert an effect until about the age of eight or nine. At about this age, children come to identify not only with other children whom they know but also with the abstraction of children in general. They begin to see themselves in opposition to adults and often find adults inferior by comparison. Peter Pan epitomizes this idealization of childhood. Like Peter Pan, children find childhood in many ways more rewarding and comfortable than what they perceive as adulthood.

At the personal level, children have a strong pragmatic bent. Psychoanalyst Erik Erikson speaks of this period as the one in which the balance is struck between the child's sense of industry on the one hand and his or her sense of inferiority on the other. If children at this stage are encouraged to work hard and to bring tasks to completion, they will establish a strong sense of industry. On the other hand, if their work is interrupted, criticized, or ignored, they may develop a sense of inferiority that outweighs their sense of industry. Children's sense of industry is reflected in the appeal of the book character Robinson Crusoe. Robinson Crusoe's ingenuity and self-reliance in furbishing his remote island world are personal ideals of childhood.

Many of the new parenting and discipline issues that arise during this developmental period have implications for grandparents as well. Children's new physical powers make it possible for them to engage in competitive sports, which presents problems as well as confers benefits. Their new intellectual abilities and formal schooling introduce issues of homework, grades, and testing. At the personal level, their sense of industry may come into conflict with adult interests and priorities. At the social level, their new allegiance to their peers can provide a challenge to parental authority and control.

✧ PHYSICAL AND MENTAL DEVELOPMENT ✧

By the age of six, children average about 3 1/2 feet in height and weigh about 45 1/2 pounds. They are now able to throw balls with accuracy and to copy numbers and letters. In addition, coincident with the eruption of their permanent teeth, children attain the power to reason syllogistically, described above. Thanks to their new levels of motor and intellectual competence, they are now able to participate in games with rules. These rule games become an important part of a child's life and contribute to many facets of development.

Games with Rules

Games with rules range from table games such as Monopoly to field games such as baseball and soccer. What is common to all of these games is that they are governed by a mutually accepted set of rules. With Monopoly, for example, a basic rule is that you throw dice and move your token as many spaces as the total number shown on the dice. Other rules regulate the purchase, sale, and mortgaging of property. Field games like baseball may have an even more complex set of rules. Try explaining a ground-rule double, for example, to someone who knows nothing of baseball.

Children acquire a number of social skills in the course of playing games with rules. For example, they learn to take turns, to be patient, and to engage in the small talk and repartee that often accompany playing games with rules. They learn cooperation as well as competition. Playing games with rules also encourages children to make up their own games with rules and to vary the rules of the games they have been playing. Creating new games and modifying old ones contribute to the child's sense of industry.

Uncoordinated Children

In playing games with rules, young people also learn a great deal about themselves. For example, children who are uncoordinated may suffer considerable embarrassment when they find it difficult to catch or kick balls, throw them, or shoot baskets. They can be teased and ridiculed by peers, and this can damage their self-confidence. To give a personal example, I was never good at ball sports and suffered excruciating embarrassment; I was often the last one chosen for a team, and my teammates groaned when I joined them. I did not learn until I was an adult that my problem resulted from a weak or "lazy" eye that made it difficult for me to assess distance and angle.

Fortunately, I was a good student, and this compensated somewhat for my athletic ineptitude. But many children do not have such compensations, and their poor performance on the playing field may be compounded by poor academic performance. Such children are particularly in need of adult support and affection. For parents and grandparents, it is important to find something the uncoordinated child can do well so he or she can have a recognized success. Finding and rewarding a child's special abilities and talents is the best thing we can do to help a child with a faltering sense of self-esteem.

Well-Coordinated Children

At the other extreme from the poorly coordinated children are those who are exceptionally well coordinated. These youngsters take naturally to sports, and the question becomes one of how much time and energy should be devoted to such activities. School-age boys now have a choice among Little League for baseball, Pop Warner for football, and PeeWee hockey. Both girls and boys can join soccer teams and take lessons in individual sports such as tennis, ice skating, swimming, and gymnastics. When done in moderation, and with coaches who are sensitive to young people's limitations and who want children to have a good time and not just win, such programs can be beneficial and rewarding.

However, when there is too much emphasis on winning and too little on the sheer joy of play with rules, the results can be less positive. Physical risks arise when children are called upon to overexert themselves and to engage in practices too strenuous for their developing muscles and bodies. A whole subdiscipline of pediatrics called pediatric sports medicine has emerged just to deal with children with sports injuries. It is now recognized, for example, that Little League pitchers should not be permitted to throw some pitches (curve balls) that are particularly taxing. And there are now international restrictions on the number of tennis competitions girls twelve to fourteen years of age can enter.

Children with Special Needs

A child with any type of physical handicap presents special challenges for parents and grandparents during childhood. Other children can be cruel without fully understanding the impact of their behavior. Perhaps the most important thing to remember for any child with a special need is just that—he or she is a child with a special need. Our language is unfortunate in the sense that we place the adjective before the noun and hence speak of the retarded child or the brain-injured child as if the retardation or the brain injury was the most significant fact about the youngster. But the child should always come first, and the adjective should be secondary. If we keep in mind that we are dealing with a child first and a special need second, we will keep the proper perspective.

Children with special needs have the same feelings and thoughts as all children. They want to be loved and appreciated by their parents and to be liked and accepted by their peers. They want to feel useful and needed and to have success with the tasks they undertake. Parents and grandparents of children with special needs will at times feel sad and angry at the injustice of a child's disability when so many other children are healthy. But life is not just, and we have to play with the cards we have been dealt. Focusing upon the positive, supporting and encouraging the child to develop his or her skills and abilities rather than bemoaning what the child doesn't have, is most helpful to the child and to the grandparents.

This, I know, is easier said than done. To help focus on the positive, I have often found it helpful for parents, grandparents, and youngsters to provide examples of famous people with comparable handicaps who did succeed. Gifted orator and diplomat Benjamin Disraeli, for example, had a speech impediment. Franklin Roosevelt was an invalid as a result of polio. And certainly the story of Helen Keller, brought to the stage and screen in the drama *The Miracle Worker,* is a testament both to what a child with special needs can accomplish and to the importance of adults who believe in the child's abilities and are willing to work hard with him or her to achieve them. It is not easy, but it is healthier for everyone to expend energies productively in helping the child realize his or her abilities rather than to waste our energies bemoaning our bad luck.

✧ EXTRACURRICULAR ACTIVITIES ✧

Games with rules are but one type of extracurricular activity school-age children participate in. While these activities can be beneficial to both physical and psychological health, they also pose risks. With respect to competitive sports, when winning becomes all-important, too few of the second- and third-string players actually get a chance to play. Warming the bench on a permanent basis is certainly not good for their self-esteem. Many of these young people do not really want to be on the field in the first place and are there only because of parental pressure. But the parents' purpose is defeated if all the children do is sit on the sidelines. Such youngsters might be better off if they were involved in an activity of their own choosing.

It is also troubling to hear stories such as the one the father of a nine-year-old boy in Little League told me. His son and teammates arrived at the playing field one glorious spring morning. The equipment was there; the parents filled the bleachers; and their opponents were suited, exercised, and ready to play. At that moment a friend of the coach arrived to say that the coach was ill and would not be able to come to the game. The boys on the team got together and talked it over. They decided they would not play. Without the coach they stood a good chance of losing, and that would put them down in the rankings. How sad that they had no interest in playing for the sake of playing but only for the chance of winning.

Nonetheless, extracurricular activities can provide a healthy avenue for grandparents to involve themselves in their grandchildren's lives. Many times grandparents can go to games, meets, and performances that the parents cannot make because of other commitments or time. Young people love to have an audience, and grandparents, in turn, take great pride in their grandchildren's accomplishments. Grandparents are, on the whole, a bit less competitive than are parents, so they are comfortable being supportive regardless of outcomes. This unconditional support is very important to the young athlete or performer and helps build that very special connection between grandparent and grandchild.

✧ INTELLECTUAL DEVELOPMENT ✧

The power to reason not only enables children to participate in games with rules but also expands children's intellectual world in many other ways. For example, at this age children attain a true understanding of quantity and number. They now understand that when a quantity changes in appearance, say when a drink is poured from a low, wide container into a tall, narrow one, there is no corresponding change in amount of liquid. Put differently, at this age children grasp that a quantity remains the same despite a change in its appearance, that it is conserved. Likewise, because children now have a notion of a unit, something that is both like and different from every other unit, they can grasp and perform the basic arithmetic operations.

Children also elaborate their conceptions of space, time, and causality. This is perhaps best illustrated by the fiction that most appeals to this age group. In books like *Winnie the Pooh* for children at the lower end of this age period and in books like *Robinson Crusoe* and *Swiss Family Robinson* for children at the higher end, there are maps, and these are intriguing to children because children now appreciate the graphic depiction of space, a significant achievement. A similar achievement occurs around the age of nine or ten when children come to grasp perspective and include this in their drawings by making figures in the foreground of the pictures large while making figures in the background small.

Stories like *Robinson Crusoe* also make much of time measurement, another new accomplishment of the school-age child. Young children may understand day and night and before and after, but they have no good idea of time units such as hours and minutes, much less years. Some young children, for example, believe that people stop having birthdays once they are fully grown. For the young child, growing older means growing taller; ergo when you stop growing, you stop aging! With the attainment of reason, however, children gradually come to understand time units and can learn to tell time from a clock face by the age of six or seven. It takes children much longer, however, to acquire a true sense of months and years. A year seems like an eternity to a child, in part because every minute and hour is so full of things that are new. On the other hand, immediate time passes very swiftly for children for the same reason—each moment brings a fresh impression. As we get older, long periods seem short in retrospect (where did the years go?), while immediate time often seems to pass very slowly, as when we are waiting in a line.

Toward the end of childhood, boys and girls acquire a new sense of causality, which is reflected in stories like *Tom Sawyer*. Tom is confronted with many practical problems that he must solve to achieve his ends, like inducing his friend to help him whitewash the fence. Practical problem solving—how to avoid detection, how to fashion a fishhook—presupposes a particular conception of causality, of what leads to what. In avoiding detection, for example, Tom has to figure out how to leave the house without being seen or heard. Such practical problem solving involves not only a concrete sense of causality, of what leads to what, but also an elaborated geographical conception of space and a solid sense of clock time.

Implications for Child Rearing

These facets of children's thinking have many practical consequences for child rearing. This is particularly true for schooling and homework. The ability to reason makes formal education, based on the inculcation of rules, possible. Formal education, at least in the United States, involves tests, grades, and homework. In turn, academic achievement often becomes a family controversy. The issue is complicated because children, even in the same family, are so different. Some children are naturally scholarly and take easily to school, to tests, to grades, and to homework. Indeed, with such children the parents' job is often to get the child's head out of the books.

At the other extreme are those youngsters who have little or no affinity for schooling. I knew one young man who went obediently to school but when asked what subject he liked best, replied, "lunch." With such young people, after making every effort to help them achieve at school, it may be necessary to accept the fact that school is not their thing. If we accept this, we have a better chance of persuading them to finish high school. We can also help them find a line of work they will like and do well. The young man described above enjoyed working in his grandfather's store in a small town, and his parents and grandfather said he could do that full time if he finished high school first.

Most young people, however, are not at the extremes but somewhere in the middle. They go to school, take the tests, do the homework, and get the grades—more or less. Here again we find wide individual differences. Some children work very hard and still get Bs and Cs. Other children work hardly at all and get the same or better grades. In our response to any particular child, we need to take into account both effort *and* ability. If a child is a B student and is really putting in the time and the effort, we should applaud that child and not demand any more. On the other hand, if a child has the potential to be an A student but doesn't put in the time, we should insist on homework being done before he or she watches television, plays computer games, or visits with friends.

The Grandparents' Role

With schooling, as with extracurricular activities, grandparents are often more relaxed than parents and are more likely to see the child's abilities and performance in a more objective light. In some cases they can gently say to parents, "She really is working hard and doing the best she can. We should give her credit for that." It is sometimes useful, too, for grandparents to remind their children of their own school experience when we see them getting too harsh on their own offspring. Parents often forget their own educational lapses when they get down on their children. And parents often see school grades as much more important for their children then they saw them for themselves. By mentioning their children's own school performance, grandparents can quietly put grades in a broader perspective.

The new level of thinking that appears in childhood has other applied consequences. For example, it can provide guidelines for buying gifts for the child. The very practical bent of this age group suggests that board games and construction toys will be very much appreciated and enjoyed. Construction sets give children great leeway in creating and building a variety of different machines and buildings. Likewise, books that involve problem solving such as adventure stories and the Nancy Drew mysteries are great favorites for this age group.

Because of children's practical bent, they appreciate being involved in adult activities. If you are involved in a do-it-yourself project such as building a deck, painting a fence, or repairing a birdhouse, involve the child. It is certainly true that, as with Tom Sawyer, when painting or any other household task is imposed upon the child as a chore that has to be done, it may be resisted. But when it is a joint activity in which the grandparent is involved, it takes on a very different value and significance. It is evidence of the meaningfulness of the work and also of the fact that the child is beginning to be accepted as a more mature and competent member of the family.

✧ PERSONAL DEVELOPMENT ✧

In human development, as in life in general, individual differences such as those described above are complex and interconnected. This is particularly true for the child's sense of self.

The child's self-conception is in fact the unique by-product of senses of physical prowess, appearance, and intellectual competence and of awareness of social acceptance and belonging. A child's sex and birth order contribute to how the child sees himself or herself. In addition, the concept of self is affected by the child's race, ethnic background, and social class.

While all of these attributes contribute to the child's sense of self, that sense is not as yet an integrated whole. It is only in adolescence that young people bring all these diverse facets of self together into a unified sense of an integrated personality, which Erik Erikson has called the "sense of personal identity."

Moral Behavior

In childhood, therefore, the child has several different senses of self. This fact has some interesting consequences for this age group. For example, it accounts for children's chameleon-like quality. When children are with adults, they are conforming and obedient—usually. When they are with their peers, they can be noisy and rebellious. In part this results from the fact that children view restraints as coming from external authority rather than from an internal set of principles as to what is proper behavior. They know that they must be quiet in the library but not in the street, but if the librarian is not present, they may be noisy in the library as well. The inhibition is not an inner rule related to the consideration of others who may be working in the library but to a rule laid down by adults. When the adult is no longer present, the rule need no longer be obeyed.

At this age level, the old adage "When the cat's away, the mice will play" certainly holds true. Again, however, we must see this behavior as a consequence of immaturity rather than the result of a moral lapse. Children at this age may be prone to tell stories or to take things that do not belong to them. While it is important to talk with children about such behavior, it is also important that we keep in mind that it is much more intellectual immaturity rather than moral depravity that accounts for the child's action.

To take a specific example, imagine you have been to

the drugstore with your grandson to buy the Sunday paper. While walking home, you find he has a candy bar that he has unwrapped and is proceeding to eat. You ask where he got the candy bar, and he replies that his friend's mother gave it to him. It was leftover candy from Halloween. You know that this kind of candy bar was openly available in a bin at the drugstore. Although you are pretty sure the candy bar was lifted and feel angry and depressed at this blatant theft, a direct accusation is probably not the best course of action.

A more productive way to proceed might be as follows: "All right, you say John's mother gave you the candy bar. It also happens to be one that was in the bin at the drugstore. When we get home, I will call John's mother and ask her about the candy bar. If she says she did give it to you, I will apologize for suspecting you. On the other hand, if she says that she did not give you the candy bar, you will take some of your own money, and we will go back to the drugstore, and you will pay for the candy bar. Then we will talk about why it is wrong to take things without paying for them."

With this procedure we accomplish several things. First of all, we do not prejudge the issue of the theft, but give the child the benefit of the doubt. Second, by suggesting that the story be put to the test, we give the child the opportunity to retract the story on his or her own. Finally, we teach the child that the way to handle a disagreement about a factual point is to get the relevant information. This way of handling the matter makes it a much more potent learning experience than if we automatically assume the young person's guilt and immediately determine punishment. Such treatment is likely only to make the child angry and resentful, and these feelings will mitigate any learning he or she might derive from the experience.

Sex Differences

Another dimension of personal development during childhood is the emergence of sex differences as a prominent divider among children. Young children are pretty much unisex. They like to play with other children, period. And while even at the preschool level, boys' play is likely to be more active and aggressive than girls' play, there is a lot of overlapping, and the boy-girl differences are not as marked as they will be later. In childhood boys tend to befriend and play with boys, while girls tend to befriend and play with girls. Such choices are reinforced by peers inasmuch as it is not "in" to be friends with a member of the opposite sex. This is not to say that the sexes are not interested in each other—they are. But the interest is one of establishing differences rather than finding similarities. It is as if this childhood period were devoted to each group's defining itself in opposition to the other. "Boys, ugh" can be heard from the girls' side as they feign disgust. And from the other side it is "Oooh, girls" as the boys feign distaste.

The Grandparents' Role

Not surprisingly, this is a period when girl grandchildren tend to gravitate toward grandmothers and boy grandchildren tend to gravitate toward grandfathers. The sense of sex role identity and allegiance is quite strong. At this age young people love to hear stories about the childhood of their own parents and grandparents, particularly if these childhood experiences were quite different from their own. In telling such stories, remember that what seemed commonplace then—working at an early age, first trips by car, and so on—will seem like fascinating adventures to the school-age child of today.

Some young people, unfortunately, seek to exploit the like-sex attachment to parents and particularly to grandparents. Some lovely young girls try to entice their grandmothers into buying them this or that piece of clothing, while some boys try to get the grandfather to underwrite a new mitt or basketball. This is a difficult issue that has several different levels. One is simply financial; some grandparents are not in a position to buy their grandchildren what they ask for. At another level many grandparents resist such demands out of a feeling that children should not be given everything they want. This is particularly difficult if the parents themselves overindulge the children.

In such situations it is most important to act upon your own principles. You might say, "Is that what you would like for your birthday? If so, I will check my budget and see whether I can manage it." This suggests that there are appropriate times for gift giving and that requests for gifts outside of those occasions will fail. If the child persists, you can simply say, "Gifts are for birthdays and holidays and special occasions, and since this is neither your birthday nor a holiday nor a special occasion, I fail to see the reason I should be giving you a gift now."

Other problems of this type emerge when the school-age child asks a grandparent for permission to do something the parents do not permit. When the grandchild is staying with you or you are at his or her house, the rules are the same. I think grandparents should abide by the rules that the parents set, even if you strongly disagree with them. It is better to discuss your disagreements with your children than to decide on your own to go against their wishes.

A somewhat different problem occurs when parents go away and the children are left with grandparents. Particularly if the children are small, this can be very distressing to the children, who may feel abandoned. It is very important to reassure children at such times that their parents do love them, and even more important, that they will come back. Of course different children respond differently, and some seem not to be bothered at all by such separations. Even with these children, however, it is important to say something about how much their parents care for them and to talk about activities they will engage in with the parents after the parents return. We also need to encourage grown children to write or call their children while they are away.

✧ SPECIAL ISSUES ✧

We need now to look at some special issues that emerge with this age group and that present problems, or at least questions, for both parents and grandparents dealing with this age group.

Lessons

Although many parents are now giving even preschool children lessons in everything from ballet to violin, the usual age for involving children in lessons is later childhood. We have already talked about team sports, where the youngster is not receiving individual lessons. Some of the questions concerning lessons are how many different activities a child should be involved in, how the activities should be selected, how much time a child should devote to them.

These are not easy questions. In general there is no need for, and no proven value to, having a grade-school child in more than three nonschool activities at any given time. A child who has one social activity, one athletic activity, and one artistic activity such as piano or guitar lessons has more than enough extracurricular activities for this stage of life. Choosing what kinds of lessons to provide for the child is more often a parental than a grandparental responsibility. Nonetheless, many grandparents are directly or indirectly involved in helping make these decisions. Generally the social activities are the easiest, usually limited to scouting, school clubs, and religious youth groups. There are many more options in the domain of sports and the arts. Wherever possible, the best, most effective strategy for choosing sports and artistic activities is to follow the child's inclinations, which are easy to discover when we observe what the child does on his or her own.

Children with athletic ability naturally gravitate to sports in their free time and will be found playing catch or shooting baskets. It is reasonable to ask such children whether they would like to join a Little League team or a soccer team or take lessons in another sport such as tennis or swimming.

Suggesting that the child get involved in sports is directive, but giving the child a choice as to what sport he or she would like to become involved in is democratic. Obviously, if we feel that it is important for a young person to be involved in some kind of sport and he or she does not wish to, we are confronted with a different problem. In some cases the child prefers to spend more time and energy in an artistic pursuit such as playing a musical instrument, drawing, or painting. Since this alternative is a healthy and productive one, it is reasonable to yield on the three types of extracurricular activities. The only proviso is to make sure the child does get a reasonable amount of exercise.

When the Child Wants to Stop. Again although dealing with a child who resists extracurricular lessons is more often a parental than a grandparental responsibility, grandparents can often contribute support and suggest options. Consider the child who has no inclination towards lessons of any kind. Such a child should be asked to make a choice and told that if he or she does not make the choice, it will be made for the child. We can also say, however, that we are going to let him or her try the lessons out. If the child likes the lessons and is getting something out of them, the child can continue; otherwise, not. It is important to set a fixed time limit for the experiment—two to three months. It is also important to leave the doors open for the future. "You may not like it now, but if you decide you want to take lessons later, we can talk about it, and it might well be possible."

Making the effort to insist that the child take the lessons at least for a given period discharges your responsibility. If the child decides not to persevere, that is the child's choice. It really is not the responsibility of parents or grandparents to hound children for years to practice for one thing or another. If children fail to take advantage of the opportunity provided by lessons, that is their decision, and we should respect it. The child may come back at some later point and say, "You should have insisted that I take lessons so now I would know how to play the piano." But your conscience should be clear.

The question of how much time children should devote to these activities depends a little on the particular circumstances of the family. Usually formal social activities such as Scout and religious youth groups meet once a week. Sports may take up several weekday afternoons and some weekend mornings or afternoons. Lessons are usually once a week, and practicing usually takes up half an hour or an hour per day. All totaled, the extracurricular activities probably take up about a dozen hours during the week. If they get much beyond this, particularly beyond twenty hours per week, the child is likely to be overinvested in these activities, and some cutting back is probably in order.

Disagreements between Parents and Grandparents. Sometimes problems arise when parents and grandparents disagree about which activities a child should engage in or how much time should be spent in these activities or both. Such disagreements rarely occur when things are going well and the child is successful in the program. It is usually when the child is unhappy with lessons that the differences between grandparents and parents emerge. Sometimes the parents want the child to persist even when he or she finds it excruciating and is making little progress. The grandparents may not agree.

The reverse can also occur. On occasion it is the grandparents who insist that the youngster persevere even when the child seems to be getting little if anything out of the activity except perhaps a headache. In both situations the focus should be on the well-being of the child. If stress—changes in mood, eating and sleeping habits, schoolwork—begins to show in his or her behavior, it is time to reduce the pressures. Unfortunately, some parents may not be ready or willing to acknowledge these symptoms of stress and may continue to press the child to take the lessons and to practice.

When parents are operating under that mind set, they are not willing to listen to anyone other than someone who supports their own view. All that grandparents can do is to provide support for the grandchildren without undermining the parents. We can reaffirm that all of us, at one or another time in our lives, have to do what others tell us to do, even when we don't like it and it seems unnecessary. We can also remind the young person that the parents are doing it for the child, not for themselves, because they want the child to have the skills when he or she grows up. It is often small comfort, but it is something.

Television

The issues of television viewing are somewhat different for school-age children than they are for preschoolers. For school-age youngsters, the amount of time watching television has been a major focus of concern. Almost everyone agrees that children watch too much television, but no one really knows what to do about it. Some recent research suggests that television may not be as harmful as we like to suppose. After examining the many studies on children and television, the investigators failed to find any clear-cut effects of television viewing on the amount of reading children do, on the time spent on homework, on attention span, or on school grades. To be sure, children who watch excessive amounts of television may be negatively affected. But such children may already be troubled, so their television watching may be a symptom rather than a cause of their problem behavior.

On reflection, these findings should not be too surprising. When comic books, radio, and the talkies first came on the scene, they were all, in their turn, held accountable for juvenile delinquency. Television is a very important and a very powerful medium, but it is also relatively new. As such, it is a convenient culprit to explain a host of social problems that probably have many, varied, and complex causes.

Baby-Sitting

As children grow older, the issue of grandparents as baby-sitters also changes. Again there are no easy answers because in some ways each family situation is unique. In some families, grandparents live nearby, the grandchildren can visit at will, and there is little problem with baby-sitting. In other families, the grandparents may live far away, and the children have to be brought by car or other transportation. Sometimes the grandparents are invited to come and stay at the child's home.

The length of baby-sitting, too, can vary from a single evening to a prolonged period.

Whatever the particular family situation, the first step before a grandparent accepts any baby-sitting invitation is to be clear about the ground rules. How long will you be expected to stay? What are the transportation arrangements? If it is to be a lengthy stay, how are the housekeeping matters to be attended to? What about the shopping, the cooking, the housecleaning? What is expected and who is going to do it? If money is involved—whether for food, outings, cleaning help, and so on—who is going to pay? All should be decided in advance.

I know this sounds a little harsh, but it will prevent hard feelings later. It is a little like a prenuptial agreement. Couples do not like to enter into prenuptial agreements because a contract seems so unromantic, so businesslike, at a time of high emotion. Likewise, when we accept a baby-sitting invitation, we do so out of love and feel a little uncomfortable talking about details. But as in a marriage, if we don't do it in the beginning, it is too late to do it later. I am not suggesting that anything be put in writing, only that the various possibilities get discussed in advance.

Of course I am not talking about emergencies, such as when the child's mother is ill, or routine visits when the parents may leave the child for a few hours while they shop or run errands. Rather, I am talking about extended stays. To illustrate, I know one widowed grandmother who agreed to baby-sit for her son and daughter-in-law for a week while they were on a combined business trip and holiday. The grandmother was happy to do it even though it meant leaving her own home, friends, bridge club, and so on. After the parents left, she found that there was little food in the house, and she immediately had to go shopping. The cleaning person came and had to be paid, which of course the grandmother did. When her son and daughter-in-law returned, they thanked her but did not ask whether she had spent any of her money. In fact, the grandmother was on a very limited income, while the son and daughter-in-law were doing quite well. It was simply thoughtlessness on their part, but the grandmother was embarrassed to raise the subject.

Adopted Children

What is the grandparents' role when the grandchildren are adopted? In my opinion no different from their role with their biological grandchildren. Here we have another case of the adjective coming before the noun when the reverse should be true. Adopted grandchildren are grandchildren first and adopted second. To be sure, it is disappointing not to have biological grandchildren, but grandchildren who have been adopted can and should become as dear to us as our biological grandchildren.

One of the issues parents have to deal with and grandparents have to be sensitive to is telling the child that he or she is adopted. There seems to be a general professional consensus that children should be told about their adopted status as early as they can begin to understand it, usually by four or five years of age. A frequent strategy for conveying this information is to emphasize the fact that the parents *chose* the child because they loved and wanted him or her. If the adopted grandchild asks the grandparents about it, we should reiterate the fact that the child was chosen and that we love him or her very much. We should say this in absolute terms and avoid any reference to or comparison with love for biological grandchildren; such a reference raises an issue and may put an idea in the child's head that should not be there.

At adolescence some adopted children become curious about their biological parents and even make efforts to find out who they are and to be in touch with them. The laws are changing in this regard, and it is now easier than in the past for adopted children to get this information. Even when the adopted children do get the information and do meet their real parents, their true allegiance almost always remains with the parents and grandparents who loved and reared them.

Childhood is the important stage of life when children come to full flower in their own right. At the zenith of this period, age ten, many children, like Peter Pan, would prefer not to grow up but to remain children forever. There is much to value and cherish in school-age children: their openness, sociability, curiosity, and practical bent. But children at this age present unique problems and require difficult decisions for parents and grandparents as well. Understanding some of the ways in which young people see their world helps us help them resolve their problems in the most positive and productive way.

CHAPTER 6

Adolescence

The adolescent period, sometimes divided into early adolescence (ages eleven to thirteen), middle adolescence (ages fourteen to sixteen), and late adolescence (ages seventeen to nineteen), marks the young person's transition to adulthood. The early adolescent years are a time of rapid growth in height and weight and also of major changes in body configuration, strength, and appearance. Equally remarkable, if less directly noticeable, are the changes that take place in the thinking of teenagers. Their new level of mental abilities vastly expands their comprehension of the physical and social worlds. Dramatic changes also occur in young people's relationships to peers. And, finally, adolescence is the period when, psychoanalyst Erik Erikson argues, adolescents put together a sense of *ego identity*—a sense of how their various abilities, traits, and propensities fit together and form a reasonably consistent personality.

Again we will look at each of these facets of development in more detail before considering some of the special problems this age group presents to parents and grandparents.

✧ PHYSICAL DEVELOPMENT ✧

Perhaps the most noticeable and dramatic physical change in adolescence is the *growth spurt,* which generally occurs about two years earlier in girls than it does in boys. For girls this spurt usually begins about age eleven, whereas for boys it usually starts about age thirteen. Although girls gain rapidly in height as well as in weight (weight increases generally precede increases in height), the gains are not as great as they are in boys. Girls gain about twenty pounds and grow two to four inches, whereas boys gain some twenty-six pounds and increase their height by an average of three and a half inches. But some young men grow as much as six inches in six months!

The fact that girls have their growth spurt earlier than boys has social repercussions during the early adolescent years. At eleven to thirteen years, many girls are likely to be taller than boys of the same age, the first time this has occurred in the course of their development. Girls also reach puberty about two years earlier than boys. These differences in rates of physical maturation explain the other physical discrepancies easily observed in most fifth- and sixth-grade classrooms. At this age level, many of the girls look quite mature in the sense of having full breast development as well as other rounded contours, while many boys retain their baby fat, short stature, and unbristled skin. At this time many girls become interested in "older men."

Perils of Puberty

The physical changes associated with puberty cause some young people considerable distress. For example, the facial configuration changes, and because the nose grows faster than the chin, some young people may look a little nose-heavy until their chin catches up with the rest of the face. Girls become very self-conscious about breast development and are eager for this to occur. There is, in our breast-conscious culture, great anxiety over breasts that are either too large or too small to fit the current societal norm of attractiveness. Some girls are eager to attain menstruation as a symbol of their new maturity. Other girls attempt to hide their budding sexuality by wearing loose clothes, T-shirts over bathing suits, and other forms of camouflage.

Boys also have concerns about their physical growth. For boys the primary concern is height. Boys who are below average in height often feel inferior and try to find ways to make themselves look taller. They may compensate in other ways, such as by becoming very competitive in sports or in academics. It needs to be emphasized, however, that there are very wide individual differences in the ages at which young people attain their growth spurt. Some young men may be short until late adolescence, when a growth spurt abruptly makes them average or above average in height.

It is important to recognize how sensitive young people are to the physical changes in their appearance. These changes are so new that teenagers have not had much time to adjust to them, and they are not really sure how other people perceive these changes. One technique I have found useful with teenagers who are anxious about features they regard as unattractive is to use examples of successful people with these traits. It is sometimes helpful to tell girls concerned about freckles that Cleopatra, belle of the Nile, had them too. I like to tell boys concerned about their height what Peter Falk, the movie actor of less than average stature, remarked: "I don't like heights. As a matter of fact, I don't even like being this tall." Young men can also be reminded that Paul Newman and Dustin Hoffman are no more than average in height.

Early and Late Maturity

Special problems can occur when a particular young person matures either earlier or later than his or her peers. In general, early maturity is more positive for boys than it is for girls, whereas late maturity is more positive for girls than it is for boys. The early-maturing boy is taller and heavier than his peers, and this tends to make him admired and looked up to.

In contrast, the early-maturing girl is out of step with both the less mature boys and girls in her age group. In addition, she is often the subject of taunts about her breasts by young boys and the object of silent or not-so-silent appraisals by older teenagers and men. And all of this is before she is really prepared to cope with these attentions.

On the other hand, boys who mature late are at something of a disadvantage with their peers. When all of his friends are tall, are shaving, and have enhanced musculature and strength, the late-maturing boy may be short and fat or spindly. He is unlikely to be able to compete well in sports and may end up as the batboy or manager of the team. Late-maturing girls, on the other hand, have had the advantage of time to grow socially before the changes in their bodies invite the attentions of young men. Girls who mature late are not pushed into premature interactions with older teenage boys, which is much more likely to happen with girls who mature early.

What Grandparents Can Do

It is easy for adults, grown accustomed to their body configurations, to regard teenagers' sensitivities to their bodies and appearance as rather self-centered and childish. In fact, however, it is quite normal for young people to feel this way, and most adults went through the very same excruciating concerns at that age. We are most supportive of young people at this stage when we recognize the seriousness of their concerns and do not make light of them or tease them about them. We help young people most by doing and saying whatever will make them feel more comfortable and accepting of the physical envelope their genes have issued them.

✧ INTELLECTUAL DEVELOPMENT ✧

Since ancient times the age of six or seven has been regarded as the age of reason. The reason meant in that expression is the logical or syllogistic reasoning outlined by Aristotle. Syllogistic reasoning, which involves a major premise (All men are mortal), a minor premise (Socrates is a man), and a conclusion (Socrates is mortal), is important, but it does not exhaust the domain of reasoning processes. Indeed, Jean Piaget, the famed Swiss psychologist, demonstrated that adolescents attain a new level of reasoning, which he called *formal operations* in contrast to the *concrete operations* of childhood.

It is not necessary here to go into technical detail about formal operational reasoning. We use formal operations all of the time without being aware of the fact. Formal operations enable us to deal with many possibilities, or choices, at the same time. Ordering food at a restaurant is a case in point. Choosing from a menu requires formal operational reasoning to the extent that it demands that we keep in mind and choose among the various possible appetizers, entrees, salads, and desserts. That is why children, who lack formal operations, have difficulty ordering at a restaurant. It also helps explain why children prefer fast-food restaurants, where the menu is simple and where they can always order the same thing.

Formal Operations and Schooling

Formal operations raise teenagers' thinking to an entirely new level. Once they attain these operations, adolescents can deal not only with multiple possibilities but also with probabilities and contrary-to-fact conditions, with historical time, and with celestial space. They can understand the allegorical significance of *Gulliver's Travels* in a way that is beyond children. The junior high school and the high school curricula reflect this new level of mental ability. It is only at these levels that subjects such as algebra, history, and literature are taught. All of these subjects require formal operational thinking to be understood.

Literary analysis provides a good illustration of formal operational thinking. True literary comprehension involves the grasp of metaphor (for example, "the shadow of your smile") and simile (for example, my love is like a red, red rose). The understanding of metaphor and simile involves the comprehension that words can have more than one meaning. Consider the following lines from Elizabeth Barrett Browning's *Sonnets from the Portuguese:*

> Let the world's sharpness, like a clasping knife,
> Shut in upon itself and do no harm.
> In this close hand of Love, now soft and warm,
> And let us hear no sound of human strife
> After the click of the shutting. Life to life—

To appreciate the simile likening the world's sharpness to that of a clasping knife and the metaphor of love as the softness and warmth of a hand requires a level of abstract symbolic thinking not available to the child but well within reach of the adolescent possessed of formal operations.

Formal Operations and Interactions with Parents

The attainment of formal operations has consequences far beyond the academic. With formal operations the teenager can think in terms of ideals and contrary-to-fact conditions. Many teenagers construct ideal parents, against whom their own parents seem most wanting. This accounts for what sometimes seems inexplicable to many parents: at ages ten and eleven, children are often obedient and respectful of their parents, but at age twelve or thirteen, many suddenly become quite critical. Whereas before, the parents could do no wrong, now they can do no right. They do not know how to dress, how to talk, or how to behave.

What is puzzling to the parents is that to the best of their knowledge, they have not changed or done anything differently to account for this turnabout—and indeed they have not. It is the teenager who has changed, who has acquired formal operations. It is well not to get too upset by these criticisms and attacks, which are as much exercises in new found abilities as genuine expressions of unhappiness. Much adolescent quarreling stems from the same impulse. With formal operations young people can marshal evidence and argue a point the way they never could as children. Consequently parents are quite right when they say that the teenager seems to be arguing for the sake of arguing—it is for the sake of exercising new mental abilities.

The teenager's readiness to criticize and to quarrel with his or her parents reflects more than the exercise of the teenager's new formal operations. These activities also provide avenues for the teenager to begin to separate from the parents and to define himself or herself in opposition to the parental view of the world and the parental way of doing things. Formal operations thus also contribute to the necessary process of separation and individuation from parents that is a major developmental task for adolescents.

Formal Operations and Peer Relations

Formal operations affect teenagers' interactions with their peers, particularly those of the opposite sex. The capacity to form ideals allows teenagers to imagine not only ideal parents but also potential mates. Hence the capacity for imagining ideals is the mental foundation for the *adolescent crush*. An adolescent's emotions also become more complicated in tandem with the change in mental abilities and account for the excruciating new feelings of attachment and longing that accompany the adolescent crush.

Such idealizations present the teenager with special problems. Many young people tend to believe that love comes in fixed quantities, that you have only so much love to distribute. Sibling rivalry, for example, often results—in part at least—from the belief that the parental love given one sibling has to be taken from the amount given to the other or others. However, when the teenager has a crush on a person of the opposite sex, he or she is confronted with a different problem. The teenager mistakenly believes that loving a member of the opposite sex necessarily means taking a certain portion of one's fixed amount of love away from parents. Because parents have been good to the teenager, such withdrawal seems ungrateful. Accordingly, the teenager feels guilty, and to assuage the guilt, often finds fault with the parents. If they are not good parents, they are not deserving of the love that is being withdrawn from them.

In part, therefore, some of the conflict between parents and teenagers is driven by the teenager's guilt over transferring love from the parents to a peer of the opposite sex. It is important, then, not to take their criticisms too seriously. Moreover, we adults—parents and grandparents—can verbalize the fact that it is all right to care about someone other than your parents. Indeed, we need to point out that love does not come in fixed quantities. In fact, it is truly a *miracle* emotion. The miracle of love is that the more you give, the more you have to give.

The attainment of formal operations affects all facets of teenagers' thoughts and action. We can see these effects in the following discussions of teenagers' social and personal development.

✧ SOCIAL DEVELOPMENT ✧

The attainment of formal operations results in three new types of social interaction that were hinted at but never fully realized in childhood: exclusivity, strategic interaction, and disillusionment.

Exclusivity

Children can be cruel to peers who are different from them in dress or physical appearance, but they seldom discriminate on the basis of personality characteristics, religious beliefs, and other mental attributes. However, such preferences do emerge in adolescence. Young people form groups as much to exclude certain peers as to include them. Social status, perhaps more than common interests, becomes a prominent dimension of adolescent group structure.

In most high schools there are four major groupings that go by different labels with succeeding generations. One group is the Brains, sometimes called Nerds, who work hard at school, get good grades, have little use for sports, and are college-bound. Another group is the Jocks, who are less interested in school than in sports, girls, and partying. The Clubbies are the popular students interested in school but also in sororities and fraternities, nice clothes, cars, parties, and exotic vacations. A final group is sometimes called the Hoods or the Baddies. These adolescents are little interested in school but much interested in cars or motorcycles, out-of-school jobs, drugs, and sex. In some cities these teenagers may be gang members.

Each group is overly stereotyped by the others, but the boundaries are generally well-known and accepted. Once identified with a particular group, it is very difficult to change to another group. One teenage girl whom I saw in my private practice moved to a new high school and was befriended by the Baddies, the only group that would readily accept new members. When she found out about the drugs and sex, she tried to leave the group and to become a member of the Clubbies. But the Clubbies would not have her, particularly after the angered Baddies spread rumors about her being pregnant and having a venereal disease. She had to change high schools in order to make a new social start.

Strategic Interactions

Another form of social exchange that emerges in adolescence is *strategic interaction*, also made possible by the attainment of formal operations. In strategic interaction we attempt to provide, gain, or conceal information to obtain some desired goal. A poker game is a good example of strategic interaction. The poker player tries to conceal information (his or her cards), to provide false information about his or her cards by bluffing, and to obtain information (read the other players' expressions and behavior to deduce what cards they hold). The aim of such strategic interaction is, of course, to win the game.

Children are not very good at strategic interaction because it presupposes thinking about other people's thinking—which adolescents can do, and children cannot. A few examples of such strategic interactions may help make this new dimension of teenage social behavior more concrete. Imagine a teenager who has been smoking against parental wishes.

Aware that his or her breath might give the indulgence away, the teenager might use mouthwash or suck on a candy breath freshener to disguise the smell. Or the teenager might leave the door of his or her room slightly ajar. This is done in full knowledge of the fact that were the teenager to shut the door, the parents would be suspicious and more likely to open it than if it was not fully closed. Teenagers can become quite ingenious in devising ways to get around parental prohibitions without the parents finding out. All such techniques are strategic interactions.

Disillusionment

The third new type of social interaction might be called *disillusionment*. The formation of crushes and the use of strategic interactions can have negative effects. The crush, for example, carries with it the TNT of its own destruction. No one can be perfect, as an idealization makes him or her out to be, and the discovery that someone we idolized is in fact only human and subject to all of human frailties can come as something of a shock. A girl who has idolized a boy from afar and who, finally meets him and discovers he uses filthy language experiences a loss of innocence that is part of the disillusionment inherent in crushes.

Disillusionment can also derive from being a victim of strategic interactions. Some boys, for example, may tell girls that they are beautiful and that they are in love, primarily to get the girl to have sexual relations. After they have attained their goal, they may not want to have anything further to do with the girl. This is an example of *strategic manipulation*, by which one young person provides false information in order to get the other teenager to do what the first person wants him or her to do. When the victim finds out that the information was presented strategically and that it was not true, the victim feels betrayed and used.

Social Interactions in the Literature for Teenagers

Teenagers' ability to engage in these higher-level social interactions is mirrored in the literature directed at this age group. The romantic novels aimed at teenage girls often deal with exclusion and disillusion. They also employ strategic interactions in the plot and the subplots. For example, a girl likes a boy and would like to get him interested in her. She accidentally-on-purpose drops her books when he is passing by so he will help pick them up and notice her in the process. The temptress wears seductive (so-called *power*) clothing as part of her strategic maneuver to capture the hero's attention. She also manages to spill something greasy on her rival's hair and dress.

Likewise, the adventure stories aimed at boys are replete with strategic interactions. The sci-fi villain disguises his voice and appearance so that he resembles a man from earth. In this disguise he enters the earth ship and quickly puts most of the crewmen out of commission. He then fakes a message to the home base as he steers the ship to his own planet. Disguises, false messages, and subterfuge all require formal operations to be used and to be understood. That is why teenagers enjoy such stories, which are still beyond the full appreciation of elementary school age children.

The new social abilities of teenagers are thus made possible by their new level of mental ability. While these new mental abilities make it possible for young people to reach new heights of intellectual achievement, they also open teenagers to both the joys of adolescent crushes and the pains of exclusion, disillusion, and strategic manipulation.

✧ PERSONAL DEVELOPMENT ✧

During adolescence young people are engaged in constructing new conceptions of themselves and of others. Chief among these constructions are the sense of personal identity, the imaginary audience, and the personal fable.

The Sense of Personal Identity

Erik Erikson describes adolescence as the period during which young people construct a sense of ego, or personal identity.

In so doing, they bring together their experiences as a son or daughter, brother or sister, student, athlete, musician, friend, rival, nephew or niece, and grandchild to form some consistent workable, meaningful whole that is their personality. The ability to put all these parts of the self together is made possible by formal operations. These operations give the teenager the mental wherewithal to incorporate the many contradictory bits and pieces of self-knowledge into an integrated theory of the self, a sense of ego identity.

The construction of the sense of personal identity takes time and effort. Often daydreaming, rock music, and talking on the phone are partly in the service of self-definition. Rock lyrics, for example, are often a stimulus for adolescents' thinking about who and what they are and what they believe in and stand for. Sometimes teenagers oppose parental values and beliefs in order to clarify their own. It is a time of testing and trying out; some young people experiment with new religions, while others go on diets or on strict regimens of exercise.

The Imaginary Audience

Along the way toward finding this sense of personal identity, teenagers construct what I call an imaginary audience. With the appearance of formal operations, teenagers are able to think about thinking, both about their own thinking and about that of other people. Usually they make a characteristic error. Teenagers are understandably very preoccupied with what is happening to their bodies, minds, and feelings. These concerns are so prominent in their own thinking that they assume that they are also the concerns of everyone about them. They thus construct an imaginary audience of persons intently observing their every word and action.

One consequence of this imaginary audience is that young teenagers become very self-conscious. As researchers, my students and I have been able to demonstrate this self-consciousness with a simple questionnaire. One of the questions for teenagers was, "You have been asked to a party that you have been looking forward to for more than a month.

Once you arrive at the party, you discover a large grease spot on your jeans or your skirt. What do you do?" Eight to ten-year-old children replied that it didn't matter and that they would stay at the party. Teenagers sixteen to eighteen years old replied that their friends would understand and that it wouldn't make any difference. But teenagers twelve to fourteen years of age gave a different type of reply. They answered that they would stand in a dark place where the stain couldn't be seen, or they would spill something else on their jeans so that it would look as if it had happened at the party, or they would go home. These answers reflected the young teenagers' extreme sensitivity to the thoughts of the audience.

While the audience can be a cause of self-consciousness and embarrassment, it can also motivate the teenager. Some young people work very hard at their studies, at sports, or at music with thoughts of the audience in mind. They are thinking about the good grades, the comments, and the applause that will result from their diligence. We all have audience fantasies such as playing a concerto at Carnegie Hall, dancing the lead in the ballet, or hitting a run with the bases loaded to win the World Series.

Yet the imaginary audience can have negative repercussions. During early adolescence in particular, young people are especially needful of the approval of the audience, which they experience as the approval of their peer group. This concern with the peer group audience can be seen in the almost slavish adherence of young teenagers to fads of dress and speech. In addition, some take unnecessary risks to win audience approval. For example, in order not to appear a sissy, a teenager may drink or smoke even against his or her natural inclinations. To be different is to invite the censure of the audience. While the audience is partly real, this age group exaggerates its importance far beyond its true significance.

The Personal Fable

Closely associated with the imaginary audience age is another construction that I call the personal fable. The fable is the belief that the person is special and unique. "If everyone is thinking about me and concerned with my words and actions, then I must be someone special. Other people will grow old and die, but not I. Other people will not realize their life's ambitions, but I will. Other people will never find that special person who is just right, but I will." Of course each person is special and unique, but no one is quite so special in life as in the personal fable.

Like the audience, the fable can have both positive and negative influences. For example, many young people attempt to write the great American novel or create a new style of painting or invent the perpetual-motion machine. These attempts arise from the conviction that nothing is insurmountable and that the striver will succeed where all others have failed. As a motivational force, the personal fable, like the imaginary audience, can direct the energies of young people and help them find their calling.

The fable can also have negative consequences. It can contribute to risk-taking. Some young people experiment with drugs not only because of their concern with the audience but also out of a mistaken belief about their invulnerability to harm. Other people, they think, will get hooked on drugs, but not they. Other people may get pregnant, but not they. Other kids will get in accidents if they drink and drive, but not they. Unfortunately, the fable gives teenagers the impression they are shielded by a cloak of invulnerability that will protect them from any and all evils.

Failures of Identity Formation

Most young people end up with a healthy sense of personal identity that allows them to get on with their lives and to use their imaginary audience and their personal fable in a realistic and productive fashion. This is not always the case. In my clinical experience, children who have not been given a clear set of values and limits can have trouble constructing an integrated sense of identity and a realistically modified imaginary audience and personal fable.

Some of these teenagers construct what I call a patchwork self of unconnected ideas, beliefs, and values. Such young people are most susceptible to the peer group and go along with whatever the group happens to condone. Other teenagers escape the problem of constructing a sense of personal identity by joining a group, such as a cult, that offers a ready-made personal identity, an admiring audience, and a fable of being elite.

✧ TEENAGE ISSUES ✧

Little children, little problems; big children, big problems. We have already touched on some of the problems teenagers present to parents and grandparents. We have seen that their self-centeredness, self-consciousness, and critical attitudes toward parents are normal expressions of this stage of life. Other problems, however, are more individual and derive from the teenager's personal strengths and weaknesses as well as from the manner in which he or she has been reared.

School Problems

Poor performance in school on the part of teenagers can result from a variety of causes.

The Seventh-Grade Slump. Many teenagers, after a successful elementary school academic career, let their grades take a tumble once they enter junior high or middle school. This probably reflects many different things, including the energy teenagers devote to adapting to their new bodies and minds. It may reflect a reaction to unceasing academic pressures, which sometimes begin in preschool. Finally, it may reflect the teenager's new awakening to the attractions of the opposite sex. I often have the impression that the sixth and seventh grades are first and foremost a place for passing notes.

If the teenager has done well academically, the seventh-grade slump need not be a cause for serious alarm. For such young people, the slump often is hardly more than a moratorium, or vacation, from academic pressures and concerns.

Most young people move out of this slump refreshed and ready for new challenges.

Female Achievement versus Popularity. That is not always the case, however. I hear from many math teachers around the country that girls who are gifted with computers often give up their talent for technology when they become teenagers. It seems that many teenage girls today are responding to a modern version of the Dorothy Parker quip:

> Men seldom make passes
> At girls who wear glasses.

Today she might have written:

> Men don't think you're cuter
> If you're good at the computer.

Despite women's liberation, some of the lore prevalent in the nineteenth century is still with us today. As Austen wrote, tongue in cheek to be sure, in *Northanger Abbey*, "A woman, if she have the misfortune of knowing anything, should conceal it as well as she can."

Even in this day and age there is a great deal of prejudice against intelligent women. Some young women still hide their brightness in order to be accepted and popular. Many parents remain ambivalent as well. They want their daughters to achieve but also to marry well, and these two wishes they feel may sometimes be in conflict.

Other Patterns. Sometimes the educational problems are more serious. This is usually the case when the teenager has never done well in school, and things just get worse as he or she progresses through the grades. Some of these teenagers are simply not academically oriented and never will be. They might best be served by a trade school or work-study program. Just as one cannot make a silk purse out of a sow's ear, one cannot make an academic out of an artisan. Such teenagers can really blossom in a trade school. It often provides them their first successful school experience.

Other young people do poorly in school because of personality issues. Although bright, they may have trouble with authority or use poor school performance to punish their parents. This sometimes happens when a teenager has been pushed too hard academically as a child and unconsciously gets back at the parents by doing poorly in junior high. Still other teenagers are simply too creative and individual to fit into the lockstep school system. Many of the latter type of young people often go on to successful careers. If they decide to go on to college or university, they do so on their own, when it is their choice and no one has made it for them. They often retain their independence, however, and may refuse to do the class work for a professor they don't like or whom they feel is doing a bad job of teaching.

What Grandparents Can Do. For grandparents, the best strategy for helping teenagers in matters educational is to avoid lecturing them. It is much more helpful to serve as a sounding board for our grandchildren. Teenagers will often talk to us when they will not talk to their parents. If we let them talk about their angers and fears, their dreams, hopes, and plans for the future, they can sort out their own feelings. Some discover that they really don't want a career. Others may discover a career is the only thing that will make them happy. We need to help them see that there are no rights or wrongs in these sorts of decisions. Only they know what is best for themselves, if they can only find that inner truth and the strength to listen to it.

Limit Setting

Setting limits, a major problem in adolescence, appears in a number of different guises.

Peer Group Limits. One of the most frequent limit-setting issues arises when a teenager befriends one or more other teenagers of whom the family disapproves. We may not like the young person's manners, mode of dress, or language. We may wonder how a nicely brought up teenager can stand to be with someone of this sort. Teen friendships can indeed be curious, but if the teenager has a good set of values and good judgment, the family should trust those values and the teenager. Youths may see the "gold in them thar hills," which often escapes their elders. Teenagers can remind us that we should not always judge a book by its cover.

On the other hand, if parents know their teenager to be weak-willed and easily influenced, the teenager's choice of friends should be a much greater matter of concern. In such cases parents have to take a much more active role and insist that the teenager terminate an unhealthy friendship. The family should tell the truth, namely, "You are too easily influenced. Instead of your being a good influence upon them, they are going to be a bad influence on you." Teenagers may fight us on this, but it is important to be firm because deep down the teenager knows that we are right and values the fact that we cared enough to confront the issue.

Curfews. Families need to take a similar stance with curfews. Time limits for young people should be reasonable and grounded in good sense. There is no need for a teenager to be out beyond midnight or a little later even on the weekend. To be sure, on special occasions the rules can be bent, but such occasions should be special. Again, it is important to remember that when parents set limits and grandparents support them, they make it clear to the young person that they care enough to take the risk of argument and confrontation.

Sometimes taking a stand has amusing consequences. One father who insisted his daughter be home by midnight often met heated resistance and reluctant submission. One evening, however, the young lady in question came home with a broad smile on her face. When her father asked why she was smiling, she said, "Oh, nothing." The father insisted on knowing, since this was in such contrast to her usual sullen demeanor at such times. "Oh," she admitted at last, "a couple of creeps came to the party, and I was the only one who had a good reason to go home!"

After-School Work. Another domain requiring limits is after-school jobs. An increasing number of teenagers are working more than twenty hours a week at after-school jobs. Often these jobs are in fast-food restaurants that stay open until late hours. Recent research, contrary to commonly accepted assumptions about the value of work, demonstrates that such jobs may not be beneficial. Since the job requires few skills and is done only to make money, it fails to teach young people the nonmonetary values and rewards of work. In addition, young people who work more than twenty hours a week do more poorly in school than do young people who put in less than fifteen hours a week on an after-school job.

Yes, work can be important and meaningful to young people, but not all work is of that sort, and not all work is equally beneficial. In particular, parents should limit the amount of time teenagers spend in after-school jobs, and grandparents should support this stand.

Activity Overload. There are other patterns to be cautious about. Many teenagers overload themselves on activities, sports, music, and academics and seem to be on an ever-faster merry-go-round. Some young people, it must be admitted, thrive on this sort of regimen. With others, however, the strain begins to show. Poor grades by a student who usually does well are often a first sign of unhealthful activity overload. Another clear sign is that the teenager no longer enjoys activities and gives evidence of frequent low mood.

When families see that the teenager is not carrying the load with ease, parents should step in. One way to handle it is to say, "Look, you really are trying to do too much, and some of the things aren't getting done well. Why don't you drop some activities and devote your time and energies to the others. I think you will do better and feel better too." This often comes as relief to the teenager, who at some level often is trying to do what he or she believes the parents expect. The teenager is often amazed to discover that no one is going to be disappointed or unhappy if he or she drops an activity or two.

What Grandparents Can Do. In this discussion I have not distinguished between role of the parent and that of the grandparent. The strategies and approaches are the same for parents and grandparents. Grandparents must intervene when the teenager lives with them or when the parents work and the grandparents have primary responsibility for the teenager's care. When you as grandparents see the parents neglecting to set limits and exercise control, you should say something to them about it. Of course you must be understanding and avoid direct criticism. One way to do this is to remind your children of the limits you set when they were young and how they are none the worse for it.

When young people are in your care, you can and should set reasonable limits. But you have to make it clear that these are your rules, to be observed while they are staying with you. In this way you do not challenge or criticize the parents but only set the rules that operate in your home. It is up to the parents to set the limits in theirs and for you to observe these if you care for your grandchildren in their own home.

Substance Abuse

Unfortunately, there are some more serious issues that today's teenagers are exposed to and that grandparents must sometimes deal with directly or indirectly. A recent University of Michigan survey found that about 70 percent of teenagers have experimented with drugs. The most used and abused drug is still alcohol. The survey also found that one out of four teenagers drinks to excess about once every two weeks. Unfortunately, many teenagers are confronted with peer pressure to use drugs just at the time when they are most vulnerable to the audience and to the fable. Even if they are well educated about the dangers of drug use, the power of peer pressure and the belief in their own invulnerability may encourage them to take risks they would not take if they were older and their belief in their own lack of vulnerability were tempered by experience.

The best thing we can do as parents and grandparents is to try to make sure that the teenager does not abuse drugs. In this connection we have to recognize that young people learn the most from the example we set. Research makes it clear that children who abuse alcohol are more likely to come from homes where parents drank to excess than from homes where the parents were restrained in their use of liquor. A teenager who comes from a home where the parents have a glass or two of wine at dinner will have a very different orientation from a teenager who sees his parents down three Scotches to unwind after a hard day at the office. The best way to prevent our children from abusing alcohol is to set an example of moderation.

It is also true that some teenagers whose parents have set a good example abuse drugs. This can happen for any number of different reasons. Often, for example, the teenager may be hit with a combination of stresses all at once and look to drugs for relief from stress—a widely shared and advertised pattern in our society. If we find that our teenager is abusing alcohol or other drugs, there are things we can do. Almost every community in the country now has a substance abuse center for teenagers. These go by different names—one is Bridge Over Troubled Waters—but they all provide, at the very least, information about where to seek help for young people who have become chemically dependent. Once a teenager begins abusing drugs, he or she requires help that is often beyond what parents and grandparents can provide. The best and most successful programs for young people with chemical dependency is some form of group therapy and/or support such as that provided by Alcoholics Anonymous (AA).

Teenage Pregnancy

More than a million teenage girls get pregnant each year in the United States. We have the highest teenage pregnancy rates of any Western society—twice that of Britain, which has the next highest rates. The average age of teenage pregnancy is declining from fifteen and sixteen to fourteen and fifteen. One reason is the increased sexual activity among teenagers. In the 1960s only about 10 percent of teenage girls were sexually active. The figure is closer to 50 percent today. In the 1960s only about 25 percent of boys were sexually active, and today that figure is closer to 65 percent. Of girls who are fourteen years old in America today, 25 percent or more will be pregnant at least once before they leave the teen years. Moreover, the rates of venereal disease among teenagers approach epidemic proportions.

Parental modeling is less of a factor in teenage sexual behavior than are peer pressure and media sexploitation. Whereas peer pressure was once opposed to premarital sex and girls worried about their reputations, today premarital sex is condoned, and young people who remain virgins become suspect. Sometimes I find that parents get caught up in this pressure and say to their teenagers, "Don't have relations, but if you do, use protection." That is a very mixed message. I think we have to say clearly, directly, and without equivocation, that sexual activity during the early and middle teen years carries serious risks. Not only is the young person not prepared emotionally for such activity, but also the research shows that the earlier a young person becomes sexually active, the more likely he or she is to experience interpersonal difficulties later.

We should counsel our teenagers to wait, that sexual activity will be more meaningful, more healthy, and more rewarding if they wait until they are more mature. Young people can learn about contraception in health classes, from literature, and so on. From us they should get a simple, direct, clear message: When it comes to sexual activity, later is better.

Again, however, despite our best efforts, we may learn that a teenage granddaughter is pregnant. I am not going to enter the debate about abortion here. Parents and grandparents should take the course of action that is in the best interests of the teenager and is consistent with their moral and religious beliefs. Whatever course of action the family takes, it is important to be supportive of the pregnant teenager and to help her feel that she is still loved and accepted. Too often, when the teenage girl gets pregnant, she feels that she is somehow so bad that she is outside the bounds of the human race. We need to assure her that she is not—that she made a mistake and that only makes her more human, not less so.

Other Problems

Other serious teenage problems include the eating disorders anorexia (dieting to the extreme of emaciation) and bulimia (alternatively binging and vomiting) as well as depression and suicide. Young people who evidence an eating disorder or depression or both are in need of professional help, and parents should seek it as soon as they suspect a problem. Most cities also have groups to help young people with eating disorders. With respect to suicide, *any* reference to it by a teenager should be taken seriously. It is very important that the parent or grandparent immediately seek professional help and guidance for the teenager who has expressed suicidal ideas.

Whatever the problem a teenager is showing, the most frequent course is for the situation to get worse, not better. That is why it is so important to take action immediately if we suspect a problem. While it is tempting to look the other way, the situation will be much worse by the time we are forced to take action. When it comes to getting help for a teenager in trouble, earlier is most certainly better.

Adolescence is a wondrous time of physical and intellectual flowering, of identity formation, and of the first romantic love. Because it is so rich in opportunities, it is also rich in emotional risks and dangers. While the majority of teenagers come through this period more mature and solid human beings, others stumble and need help to find their way. If we, as parents and grandparents, are there to help them find that way, to let them see that they are only human, we can get even those who stumble to walk proud and upright once more.

CHAPTER 7

Family Stress

The family in the United States is dramatically different than it was barely a quarter-century ago. The once-dominant nuclear family—mother, father, and two or three children—is now, if not a rarity, at least a minority. Single-parent families, two-parent working families, and blended families of remarried parents and their children from former marriages have become the norm. Such a rapid change in family structure is unprecedented. These new family configurations make extraordinary demands for adaptation upon family members.

✧ STRESS IN CONTEMPORARY SOCIETY ✧

If the first half of the twentieth century has been called the age of anxiety, the second half could well be called the age of stress. The difference is important. Anxiety, which is self-generated, expresses the unconscious fear of being unable to control oneself or one's surroundings. Stress, in contrast, comes from without; it tests our ability to cope with external demands. To be sure, there was plenty of stress in the first half of this century, and there is more than enough anxiety in the second. The difference is relative at best. Nonetheless, the first half of the century saw less rapid social change than the second. Social change promotes stress, while social stability is comparatively more conducive to anxiety.

The Stress Response

In the broadest sense, stress is coincident with life. There can be no life without adaptation to external demands. Some of these demands come from the physical environment. Changes in temperature, for example, require that we add or remove clothing. The social environment also makes demands. As parents or grandparents, we expect children of a certain age to toilet, dress, and feed themselves. Children respond to these demands by learning the requisite skills. In general, learning is the most common way of dealing with social demands for altered behavior.

In the narrower sense, however, stress refers to *extraordinary* demands for adaptation. It is in this narrower sense that we tend to refer to stress in everyday speech. Many years ago the American physiologist Walter Cannon described in his book *Bodily Changes in Pain, Hunger, Fear and Rage* the body's resources for dealing with extraordinary demands for adaptation. Cannon wrote that whenever we are confronted with extreme demands for adaptation, the body undergoes a set of changes preparatory for *fight* or *flight*. The blood pressure rises, the pulse rate increases, adrenalin is pumped into the bloodstream, and breathing becomes more rapid. All of these reactions prepare the body for an unusual expenditure of energy.

The stress reaction was essential in prehistoric times, when men and women were frequently threatened by wild animals as well as by hostile tribes. Even in modern society, the stress response can be very welcome. It provides an extra burst of energy when we are running to catch a young child before he or she steps into the street. Likewise, the stress reaction enables us to swim faster when we are going out to rescue someone in trouble.

The Stress Response Today

In contemporary society, however, the stress reaction is not a healthy reaction to many of the stresses we encounter. When a person is turned down by an employer after asking for a raise, neither fight nor flight is an appropriate reaction. Likewise, when a student fails to get into the college of his or her choice, there is no one to fight and no place to run. It has to be emphasized that positive as well as negative events can evoke the stress response. Getting a raise, receiving a proposal of marriage, and winning a coveted contest or prize can all evoke the stress reaction.

Stress is our constant companion in contemporary life. Consider just a few of the stresses that are universal in urban societies all over the world. Traffic congestion is a given in almost every modern city from Paris to Tokyo. Sitting in a car for hours on end and moving at a snail's pace is stressful. This is particularly true if you are going to a job, meeting, or class where you are expected to be on time. Likewise, modern technology is wonderful except when it doesn't work. The more technology, the more possibilities of failure. So-called computer viruses can be a serious source of stress to computer operators and to managers when information is lost or turned into gibberish.

✧ THE ROLE OF PERSONALITY ✧

Whether or not we respond with the stress reaction to particular circumstances depends upon the situation and our own personality. If, for example, we have prepared ourselves for being turned down for a raise, our reaction will be much different than if we have already decided how to spend it. Likewise, if we place little importance on winning, our reaction when we do win is less powerful. In short, how we react to external demands is always determined, in part at least, by our own personal way of perceiving those demands. One person's stress can be another person's recreation.

✧ STRESS DISEASES ✧

What happens, then, when our stress reaction is aroused and we have no way to expend the energy reserves made available to us? Hans Selye, the physiologist who first described the negative impact of stress, has said that it can result in a number of stress diseases such as high blood pressure, headaches, and ulcers. More recent research has suggested that unrelieved stress reactions also affect the immune system. When we are under constant stress, we are much more susceptible to disease of all sorts than when we are not. Unrelieved stress, therefore, can be a serious health hazard.

✧ TWO SOURCES OF FAMILY STRESS ✧

Unfortunately, it is not only modern society that contributes to stress. Family relationships can also be stressful.

There are two basic sources of family stress: those we experience outside the home and bring back with us and those that originate in the family relationships themselves.

We do not leave the stresses we experience outside the home behind us when we return. Rather we bring these stresses home with us. A child who has been scolded by a teacher at school may come home angry at his mother. A mother who failed to meet a deadline at work may not be responsive to her children's demands for attention when she gets home. A father who has had a flight canceled and had to miss an important meeting may snap at his wife. When we are stressed, we tend to stress those closest to us.

Other family stresses are produced by the relationships within the family. Every human relationship germinates the seeds of conflict as well as harmony. The newness, range, and variety of contemporary family styles, together with our inexperience in dealing with them, makes the potential for conflict in these relationships even greater than it was in the past.

It is impossible to discuss all the stresses that we encounter outside the home, but we can look at some of the stresses that arise from contemporary family configurations and suggest some healthy ways to deal with them. If we reduce some stresses within the family, we also help family members deal more effectively with stresses they encounter in the outside world.

✧ FAMILY RELATIONSHIPS ✧

Attachment is a basic source of stress. Whenever we are attached to a person, place, or thing, we become subject to stress. Indeed, the Stoic philosophers as well as those of Eastern religions such as Buddhism counseled divesting ourselves of attachments in order to attain a serene (unstressful) life. Nonetheless, attachments are part of life, and most of us cannot do without them. When we become attached, we make ourselves vulnerable to stress. Separation from loved ones and danger and harm to them become a stress to us. Likewise, our loved ones being at times unfeeling and insensitive, can also cause stress. To understand how this happens, we need to look at how these attachments come about.

Attachment of Parents

Children become attached to those who care for them. Attachment means that the child prefers the parents to all other adults. In the early years of life, the child feels safe and secure in the presence of the parents and frightened and uneasy when the parents are gone. Parents bond to their children in a similar way. They see the child as their creation and their responsibility. In addition, the child's preference for them and obvious pleasure in their company cements the attachment. There seems to be a strong component of instinct in the bonding process both from child to parent and from parent to child.

Attachment to Grandparents

The attachment of children to their parents and the attachment of parents to their children is easily explained. When we turn to the attachment between children and their grand-parents, however, the explanation is not so simple. Grand-parents are not, or not usually, the prime care givers of the child. They may not, and most often do not, live in the same house or neighborhood. Moreover, children do not intellectually understand the biological kinship until they are seven or eight. And yet many children are well attached to their grand-parents at an early age, and many grandparents feel strongly bonded to their grandchildren. How is this possible?

The answer in my opinion is much the same as the one we give to explain the attachment of a child to a parent when the parent is not the primary caregiver. Many young children today spend more of their waking hours with caregivers in daycare centers or with baby-sitters at home than they do with their parents. Nonetheless, the children attach to their parents and not to the caregivers. Clearly, the amount of time spent caring for a child does not determine its attachment.

Emotional Commitment. Much more important, it appears, is the caregiver's emotional commitment to the child. This commitment is communicated in the caregiver's words, body language, and overall responsiveness to the child. Apparently infants are well programmed to read these nonverbal communications. Infants apparently discriminate very easily between caregivers who are simply looking after them and those who are committed to them for life. It is the ways in which parents and grandparents talk to the infant, hold the infant, and smile at the infant that tell the infant that this is the person in whom to invest.

When grandparents are with their grandchildren, they use the same communication system as parents. Watch a grand-parent with an infant grandchild. The grandparent holds the baby close, looks down, smiles, coos, and communicates love and pleasure in many different nonverbal ways. The baby responds to these grandparental nonverbal cues in the same way that it responds to similar cues from the parents. The infant attaches to his or her grandparents because the grand-parents communicate their love and commitment to the child.

Generativity. But why do grandparents attach to the grandchild? This seems like one of those questions to which the answer is so obvious that it really doesn't need to be asked. Of course grandparents attach to their grandchildren. They are the grandchildren after all, flesh of the flesh, although the grandchild is only half of each pair of grandparents biologically—and at least some grandparents are not too happy about the other half! Moreover, while there is only one set of parents, there are two sets of grandparents, which might certainly dilute the attachment.

In most cases, grandparents are most certainly attached to their grandchildren. How does this come about? At least part of the answer is suggested by Erik Erikson. He argued that once adults reach the age of grandparenthood, they must deal with the issue of *generativity* (devoting our time and energy to the nurturing of the next generation) versus *stagnation* (continuing to be fully absorbed in our own lives and pleasures). As we move toward retirement, our values change. Most of us have already made whatever mark on life we are going to make, and now we have a choice. We can continue to pursue our own career or life goals, or we can move outside ourselves. If we can decenter from ourselves, we often become concerned with helping young people with their lives, a way of attaining generativity. On the other hand, if we continue to pursue our own goals without regard to the next generation, we tend to stagnate and become increasingly self-engrossed.

The attachment of grandparents to grandchildren is one expression of generativity. Our attachment to our grandchildren expresses our concern for their future and our commitment to helping them along in life. That attachment and concern are, of course, heightened by the fact that they are our grandchildren and are related by blood. But the blood relationship is really not enough. This is true because those grandparents who have chosen stagnation over generativity show little attachment to their grandchildren. Such grandparents are too self-absorbed to become significant figures in the lives of their grandchildren.

Grandparent-Parent Attachments

The birth of grandchildren not only introduces new attachments but also affects many existing attachments, particularly those between parents and grandparents. In the most usual case, this relationship is strengthened by the appearance of a grandchild. This is most often true for the grandmother-mother relationship. In the process of becoming a mother, many women begin to appreciate—in ways they never did before—what their own mothers experienced. Their understanding of their own mothers is deepened and softened. Thus, becoming a mother brings many women closer to their own mothers.

Something similar but lesser occurs between grandfather and father. A number of studies suggest that with the birth of a child, fathers acquire a new sense of responsibility and commitment to family. As a consequence, they may now more fully appreciate those qualities in their own fathers. They may also forgive their fathers for not being available as often as they would have liked. Indeed, many contemporary fathers choose to spend more time with their children than their fathers did with them.

Grandmother-Mother Conflict. In some cases the appearance of a grandchild can create problems between parent and grandparent. This is particularly true when the parent-grandparent relationship has not been a happy one. For example, in her book *Her Mother's Daughter,* Marilyn French describes the resentment of a woman against her mother, who shows the granddaughter much more love and affection than she has ever shown her own daughter. Such feelings and resentments run very deep and may have destructive consequences. If the mother is really immature, she may try to punish her own mother by not allowing her to be with the baby. Such situations are stressful for everyone involved.

The Mother-in-Law. Another problem of this sort centers on the age-old mother-in-law relationship. One consequence of the enhanced attachment between mother and grandmother is that the father's mother often becomes the excluded member of this feminine trio. My own impression is that the presence of the husband's mother actually helps make possible the closer relationship between mother and grandmother. What happens is that many of the negative feelings and traits that once separated mother and grandmother are now directed toward and attributed to the mother-in-law. Both mother and daughter can find fault with her and unite against a common enemy.

A mother-in-law cast in this negative role does not have many options because she is not dealing with facts and logic but with feelings and emotions. Everything the mother-in-law does is likely to be misinterpreted, seen in the most negative light. Neither self-defense nor efforts at ingratiation have any effect. Often the best strategy is for the mother-in-law to get on with her own life. If she spends too much time worrying about the daughter-in-law and her mother, they will have succeeded in making her unhappy. She should enjoy her grandchildren when she can and not fret about the rest.

To be sure, this is not always the case. Many times daughter and mother-in-law get on better than mother and daughter—a situation, by the way, that has its own problems. It must also be admitted that not all mothers-in-law are innocent. The point is that we have to be careful about generalizations. Families are just too variable to cast any one member into a stereotypical role.

Grandparent-to-Grandparent Relationships

In the best of all possible worlds, the sets of grandparents are similar enough in values, tastes, and interests to become friends. When this happens, they can be supportive of each other, of their children, and of their grandchildren. In my experience, however, the best of all possible worlds is not the most probable world. In too many cases, the grandparents do not get along. Sometimes it is an all-around mutual dislike. In other families one or the other grandparent is seen as impossible.

When the grandparents don't get along, problems in dealing with the grandchildren may arise. Most often this takes the form of what might be called *grandparent rivalry*. In many respects grandparent rivalry is the counterpart of sibling rivalry. Sibling rivalry is the contest between siblings to win the most affection from their parents. Grandparent rivalry is the contest between two sets of grandparents to win the most affection from their grandchildren.

In many cases the mother's parents have the advantage in this competition because of the enhanced attachment between the women. For example, the mother's mother may be asked to stay with the couple during the mother's lying-in period. Sometimes one set of parents entices the couple to live near them and away from the other parents. This gives the closer parents much readier access to and more influence upon the grandchildren than the other set. Here again, there is little the more distant parents can do. Not getting upset at the unfairness, but enjoying the grandchildren when you can, is often the best strategy. If you make clear that you are not going to enter a contest for the grandchildren's affection, the other grandparents may relax.

Sometimes grandparents' rivalry is fought on the field of presents and outings. Some grandparents are more affluent than their rivals, and they may try to win the grandchildren with expensive gifts and elaborate vacations. Here again, there is little point in engaging in such a competition, and it is not in the best interests of the grandchildren. The most effective strategy is to ignore what the other grandparents are giving. Our gifts should reflect what we can afford and what is developmentally appropriate for the child and value-appropriate (for example, books as opposed to war toys) for us. As the grandchildren mature, they will appreciate gifts of this kind much more than presents chosen primarily to win their affection.

✧ DIVORCE AND REMARRIAGE ✧

Family patterns in the United States, as in the rest of the industrialized world, are changing. Some of these changes are already well known. Nuclear families (two parents, two or three children, one parent working) now make up less than 10 percent of family configurations. Two-parent working families, single-parent families, blended families (remarried parents with children from previous marriages), and men and women living alone are now the dominant domestic arrangements.

The family has changed in other ways as well. On the average, families are much smaller today than in the past. Parents with a single child or with two children are the rule. This means that children today grow up with no siblings or with fewer siblings than was true in the past. At the same time, thanks to changes in health and longevity, many more children than in the past have living grandparents. Contemporary family configurations, therefore, are likely to contain more adults than children. This is the reverse of what was true in the past.

Parental Divorce and Remarriage

One of the constants of contemporary family life is the frequency of divorce. The divorce rate in the United States (according to *Current Population Reports*) is currently between 40 percent and 50 percent, which is to say that couples marrying today have about a 50 percent chance of staying together throughout the life cycle. About 80 percent of those who divorce remarry. Remarriage generally occurs within three years of the divorce, and men are more likely to remarry than are women. Of those who remarry, about half will divorce a second time.

It is well for grandparents to consider some of the possible implications of these patterns. For example, when a mother or father divorces and then remarries, the children automatically acquire a third set of grandparents. This necessarily complicates the whole grandparent scenario. The parents of the divorced spouse do not disappear from the scene, for it is their grandchild. The nonbiological grandparents have to be careful not to intrude on the biological grandparents' relationships. On the other hand, they may have more actual responsibility for caring for the child or children, particularly if their daughter has remarried a man with children.

Sometimes the new parent does not allow the biological grandparents to visit the grandchildren. A deeply saddened grandfather, 61-year-old Robert Ross Wylie, describes the painful consequences of such separation in *Age Wave*, by Dychtwald and Flower (Los Angeles: Jeremy P. Tarcher, Inc., 1988).

> Melissa had big blue eyes, blonde hair and a wide smile of bright sunshine. She could get anything she wanted from Grandma and me. The drumstick at Thanksgiving seemed almost as big as she was. She grasped it in her tiny hands and had such fun trying to bite into it with next to no teeth at all, and when it slid out of her hands, she squealed with sheer delight. Then, in her swing chair, she made happy little sounds as a music box lulled her to sleep. I loved to hold her when she napped.
>
> The day came when I picked up what was left . . . a broken toy car without front wheels . . . the leg of a doll . . . There was no more music from the music box, no golden laughter. Only silence. I looked out the window, and the window started to blur. I choked back the tears. Grandpas aren't supposed to cry.

That was written when Wylie's granddaughter was three. He and his wife have not seen her since. She is now eleven. Because this sort of experience has become increasingly common, grandparents have organized to combat it. As a result of the work of grandparent groups such as Grandparents-Children's Rights, Inc., every state, though not the District of Columbia, has in the last decade passed laws allowing grandparents to petition for visitation rights.

Blended Families

Family relationships can get even more complicated. A not-unusual configuration occurs when one parent remarries and has another child with the new spouse. The grandparents now have two grandchildren sharing only one parent. If, as happens too often, the divorced couple do not get along, the role of the grandparents becomes rather difficult. Both parents are likely to watch the grandparents very closely for any signs of favoritism, and grandparents have to be careful in this regard.

In my experience, the critical issue in all of these family configurations is *loyalty*. The real question when there has been a divorce and remarriage is, Where do our loyalties lie? In most instances our loyalties are with our own son or daughter, but if we have a good relationship with our son-in-law or daughter-in-law, we may not want to sever it. On the other hand, our own child may take it as a sign of disloyalty to him or her if we do continue to maintain contact with the divorced spouse. The majority of such problems are most intense around the time of the divorce. After three or four years, the majority of divorced couples become, if not more friendly, at least less hostile.

With this knowledge in hand, we can maintain our relationship with the divorced spouse with the understanding that this will eventually be accepted, perhaps even appreciated, at a later point. In the meantime it is best to be honest about our intentions. We might say, "I know you are very angry now, but your former spouse has always been very decent to us and we really want to maintain our relationship. But this has nothing to do with our love for you. We think you will feel differently about this later."

When dealing with grandchildren, the loyalty issue also arises. This is particularly the case when children from two different marriages are involved. Children, no less than their parents, are concerned with loyalty. They are on the lookout for even the most minute signs of favoritism. Unlike siblings, who might attribute such favoritism to special personal qualities, stepchildren are likely to attribute it to family ties. We have to do whatever we can to dispel such beliefs. At the same time, we have to be ourselves and not be walking on eggshells.

The most important consideration in such family configurations is to be aware of the loyalty issue and to deal with it openly and frankly. Saying something like "You are our grandchild and we love you, period," may help dispel children's worries about our loyalty. At the same time, we may indeed like some of our grandchildren better than others. We are only human, after all. But we should make every effort to be fair and equitable in our treatment of each of the grandchildren.

Grandparent Divorce and Remarriage

A somewhat different family pattern emerges when it is the grandparent who remarries. Here again the issue is often one of loyalty. Unfortunately, grandchildren may be quite outspoken about their loyalties and tell the new grandparent in clear language that the former grandparent was preferred. Children can be cruel, often because they have been hurt. That is why it is so important to prepare them in advance for any move of this kind. I know of one teenager who was shattered when her grandfather remarried without telling her about it and simply appeared one day with his new bride.

Sometimes we get so caught up in our own lives we forget the impact we have upon others. Spending some time with our grandchildren explaining the situation and introducing them in advance to the grandparent-to-be often prevents a lot of unhappiness later.

Grandparent remarriages present still another variety of the loyalty issue. This is particularly true if each of the grandparents has children and grandchildren. It is not only the children and grandchildren who encounter loyalty problems. When grandparents remarry, they have to deal with their loyalties to their own children vis-à-vis those of the new spouse. This can even be a cause of marital conflict and stress if one grandparent feels the other is being partial to his or her own. None of these loyalty problems are insurmountable, but they do have to be faced and talked about. Otherwise they can become an ongoing and increasing source of conflict and stress.

Generally, when there has been a divorce, the father is more likely than the mother to remarry, most likely to a never-before-married younger woman. This means that divorced women with children have a reduced probability of remarriage. As a result, one effect of our high divorce rate is that there are many more single-parent families today than there were several decades ago. Single-parent families pose such special problems for grandparents that we need to look at them in a little more detail.

In 90 percent of the cases of divorce with children, mothers are given custody of the children. Because women on the average earn less than men, this generally results in a lowered standard of living for the mother and offspring. Accordingly, a divorced daughter with children may add to grandparents' financial obligations. If the daughter is young, she and the grandchild may actually come to stay with them for a while. In a 1986 national survey, three out of ten grandparents said that in the case of divorce the grandchild had come to live with them, often accompanied by his or her parent.

Although grandparents usually accept this eventuality with good grace, it can be stressful. I talked with one couple who were really looking forward to the husband's retirement. They had purchased a motor home and had an itinerary all planned out. Both of them were eagerly looking forward to crossing the country and visiting places like Niagara Falls and the Grand Canyon, which they had never seen. Shortly before they were to leave, however, their daughter announced that she was getting divorced and was coming home with her baby daughter.

Because their daughter did not have professional skills, she could not command a high salary. Moreover, she was getting no alimony and only a small amount of child support. The parents realized immediately that they would have to help her financially. Only after exploring the grim child care options, however, did they realize that they would have to help her in other ways as well. So the trip was indefinitely postponed as the grandmother took over the care of her granddaughter while the daughter worked. While the grandparents loved the baby, it was a bitter disappointment to have to give up the trip.

Our children may have complaints about the new living arrangements as well. In another family I counseled, a successful professional woman with a daughter twelve and a son four moved back with her parents after her divorce. She found that they once again treated her as they had before she was married. They wanted to know whom she was going out with, scolded her for staying out too late, and even monitored her clothing. They loved the grandchildren and did a marvelous job of looking after them before and after school but needed to recognize that their daughter was a grown woman quite capable of running her own life.

Coping with a Child Who Has Returned to the Nest

All that we can really do when our newly divorced children return to live with us is try to make the best of it. We must help our children get on with their lives in any way that we can, but we also have to be discriminating. In some cases, having our child and our grandchildren come to live with us is a real blessing. It gives us a chance to play an important role in the lives of our grandchildren, and this can be very gratifying. If our own child is thoughtful, appreciates what we are doing, and does not take advantage of the situation, it can be a happy, fulfilling arrangement for everyone involved.

But not every situation is like that. Sometimes our children are immature and take heedless advantage of our generosity rather than appreciate what we are doing to help. In such cases we have to be very firm. We need to make it clear from the beginning that our help is a temporary arrangement and that we have every expectation that eventually our son or daughter will be independent. We will try to be there to back our child up, but we need to get on with our lives as well.

This may seem cruel and hard-hearted to many readers,

but the alternative is actually much crueler. If we coddle our grown children who have not attained a mature ability to be independent, we encourage unhealthy dependency. We are not going to be around forever, and if we do not foster independence now, we may not be around to do it later. If we are too accommodating, we can be taken for granted. I know of at least one divorced daughter living at home whose abuse of her parents' good nature is out of control. This young woman makes dates and arranges her social calendar without even discussing it with the grandparent baby-sitters in advance. If we are too accommodating, we run the risk of being exploited.

Nor should we expect to be thanked for our efforts. It is a perverse fact of human nature that when someone does a great deal for us, we often turn gratitude upon its head. Somehow they did us a favor, and we owe them gratitude. A number of grandparents have told me stories of this sort. One couple took their son and his two children into their home while the son was putting his life back together. In addition to providing food and shelter, they did a lot of baby-sitting. The son was not grateful for all that his parents had done. Rather, he was unhappy that his father didn't let him use the family car whenever he wanted it. Even though such ungratefulness is common enough, it can be difficult to take. So while we should do everything we can to help our children, we have to be clear that this is not a permanent arrangement.

Coping with Our Grandchildren
When They Live with Us

Our relationship to our grandchildren is also somewhat different when they are living under our roof. This usually presents no problems if grandparents and mother or father are in accord with regard to child-rearing practices, but it can be difficult if our concept of caring is quite different from that of the mother or father. What do we say to a parent who overindulges his or her child and who is afraid to set any limits? Certainly we have to set limits of our own, and if these are not enough, we really need to talk with our son or daughter.

This can be difficult. Some sons and daughters will take any discussion of this kind as criticism and intrusion and threaten to move out. With this approach they can play on our guilt and on our attachment to the child. Again, however, it is often much kinder to be tough than it is to be gentle. We need to take a stand and stick to it. It is important to say that children need limits and that it is unhealthful for them not to have rules to live by. While we love mother or father and child and want them to stay with us, some rules have to be followed if we are to live together in a harmonious way.

Such discussions are never easy, but it is much better to have them than to let unspoken resentments build up on both sides. When such buildups occur, the result is usually an explosion, which is not good for anybody.

✧ CHILDREN AND DIVORCE ✧

We need to look a little more closely at the effects of divorce upon children. Obviously, each divorce is different, but there are some common effects that can be pointed out. These can aid our understanding of children who are experiencing this traumatic event. The effects will vary with the age of the child, with the sex of the child, and with the maturity and good sense of the parents. Perhaps the best information we have on the short- and long-term effects of divorce on children comes from the work of Judith Wallerstein, which she has recently published in the book entitled *Second Chances* (New York: Ticknor and Fields, 1989).

Infants and Divorce

When a divorce occurs early, before the child is two or three years old, there is very little trauma. In the usual course of events, it is the father and not the mother who leaves. The young child's primary attachment is usually to the mother, and this remains constant. Moreover, young children have a very limited understanding of time and relationships, so they really cannot comprehend the situation. Children do not fully appreciate the meaning of divorce on an intellectual plane until about the age of seven or eight. Emotionally, of course, they understand it much earlier.

Preschool Children and Divorce

If the divorce and separation occur during the children's preschool years, particularly the ages of four and five, the effects are often more severe. In part, this is a result of the fact that young children have limited concepts of space and time. Wallerstein points out that young children do not really understand the time involved in the statement, Daddy will come next Monday. Because they have a limited understanding of distance, they also worry about finding their way home from Daddy's house to Mommy's house.

Young children often show strong emotional reactions to divorce. They may attack their younger siblings or bite their playmates. Sometimes they resume wetting the bed after having been dry for more than a year. Some young children believe that something they did drove the parent away. They may try to atone by giving away a much-loved toy. Some young children even become accident-prone and unconsciously punish themselves in this way.

As grandparents, we need to reassure our grandchildren of our love for them and if possible increase the frequency and length of our visits after the parents have separated. We cannot substitute for the absent parent, but we can provide strong support for our grandchild and the custodial parent.

Early School Years and Divorce

Wallerstein found that children in this age group who experienced divorce were most concerned about losing the noncustodial parent forever. Often they worry about being replaced in the parent's affection by another adult, a child, or even a pet. In addition, they may also begin to fantasize that the separated parent will return at some later time. Wallerstein found that many children at this age showed a year-long decline in quality of schoolwork. She observed that when the mother is the custodial parent, boys experience an intense, painful longing for their fathers. Sometimes children at this age see divorce as a fight and feel they must take sides. Conflicts of loyalty are intense at this age level.

As grandparents, you can be supportive of children in the early school years by encouraging them to talk about their feelings. You should avoid talking about the divorce itself, about who was most at fault, and so on. Children will make their own assessment on those issues. What you can say is something like, "Many children are quite unhappy when their parents divorce. It is scary. So whenever you want to talk about it, I'll be very ready to listen." You can also say (but only if we know that it is true), "I'm not sure about a lot of things, but I am sure that your mother and father love you very much."

Later School Years and Divorce

Children between the ages of nine and twelve have a strong need for family stability and security from which they can take on new intellectual and social challenges. Wallerstein found that children at this age became very angry at the parents because the divorce was so devastating to their projects and plans. Many children at this stage become particularly angry at the parent they regard as responsible for the divorce and may join forces with the other parent. Together the parent and child may engage in behaviors and activities designed to anger, humiliate, and embarrass the other parent.

Not infrequently, too, children at this age level will attempt to assume an adult role and play the part of either companion to or parent of the custodial parent. The child may prepare meals and clean the house and may come to feel that the parent is dependent upon such care. This can put a lot of stress upon the child.

Grandchildren at this age level who experience divorce need your support, you must be careful not to join forces with the child and one parent against the other parent. This can present problems if your unwillingness to attack the other parent is seen as taking his or her side. Sometimes it is even necessary to say, when you are asked to take sides directly or indirectly, that you will not do so.

You can help children who are assuming too adult a role with respect to the custodial parent. It is important to be positive and to say how much you admire the child's efforts and how helpful they are, then remind the child that he or she is still a child and that it is okay to be taken care of and to allow grandparents to do just that.

Teenagers and Divorce

In some ways the age group that is hit hardest by divorce is that of teenagers. Young teenagers in particular are just beginning to develop an interest in the opposite sex and to think about love and marriage. Early adolescents tend to idealize people and relationships. It is quite shattering to their idealization of love and marriage to learn that their parents are going to divorce.

Wallerstein found that the adolescents she studied wondered whether they would repeat their parents' failure. They were also disturbed to see the parents' emotional and sexual problems at a time when they were going through such troublesome emotional and sexual conflicts themselves. Many of the teenagers in her study saw the divorce as a kind of betrayal. They felt that they should not have to cope with their parents' problems when they had so many of their own.

If we have the opportunity, we can help the teenager cope with the divorce. We can reassure him or her that, yes, some people do divorce, but many do not. We should also emphasize that what the parents do is not necessarily what their children do. If we have remained married, we can point out our circumstance to them. The fact that we remained married did not prevent our children from divorcing. In the same way, the parents' divorce does not mean that the children will do likewise. In fact, parental divorce may make the children work harder to ensure that their marriages will remain intact.

Regardless of the age at which the divorce occurs, it is always stressful for children. The fact that divorce is more common today does not really help much. If you break your leg, it doesn't hurt any less or take any less time to heal if your friend has broken a leg as well. Divorce hits at children's sense of security and challenges their view of themselves as good people and of the world as a reliable place. We need to do everything we can to assure our grandchildren that they are still loved and that they will be cared for and looked after. Grandparents whose own marriage is strong can be a very stabilizing security base for grandchildren if their parents divorce.

CHAPTER 8

Social Stress

In our day, rapid social change, widespread social unrest, fast-paced technological innovation, and intense international economic competition have become major sources of stress to families. The social dynamics that operate in our society such as the two-parent working family, technology, the media, education, and religious institutions can be supportive of families but they can also contribute to family stress.

✧ TWO-PARENT WORKING FAMILIES ✧

More than 50 percent of families with children under the age of six have both parents in the work force. It is estimated that by the beginning of the next century, more than 90 percent of women will be employed full or part time. Two-parent working families have become the norm rather than the exception. While women have always worked within the home, the new family configuration of both parents working outside the home introduces some new forms of stress and exacerbates others.

The Child Care Crisis

More than six million children below the age of six are now cared for outside the home on a part-time or full-time basis. The entrance of large numbers of mothers into the work force has created a child care crisis. This crisis does not arise from the character of contemporary mothers but rather derives from social shortsightedness. The movement of women into out-of-home employment came about without adequate provision for looking after the children while the mothers were at work.

Finding quality child care has become a major source of contemporary family stress. Even when parents are fortunate enough to find quality child care, they still worry about how the child is getting along while they are at work. In addition, parents have to be concerned about what will happen if the child gets sick. Many child care facilities will not accept children who are sick for fear they will infect the other children. Yet many employers are not willing to accept a child's illness as sufficient cause for a parent to stay home from work. Not surprisingly, nearby grandparents may be called upon under these circumstances, which in turn may put stress on them.

For grandchildren who are of school age, grandparents may also be called upon to provide care before and after school. Parents know that children need supervision when they come home from school and the parents are not yet home from work. While some schools and communities provide such care, it is still relatively rare. So it is quite natural for children to go to their grandparents' homes after school if the grandparents happen to live nearby. While having grandchildren stop by after school can be a pleasure when it happens occasionally, it can be stressful if it becomes routine.

As two-parent working families have become the norm in our society, many grandparents have had to take over a larger share of child care than in the past.

✧ TECHNOLOGY ✧

It is truly astonishing to realize that most of the contrivances we use in our everyday lives were invented in this century. Telephones, radios, televisions, computers, microwaves, jet planes, Fax machines, and many more conveniences have all been introduced within the last one hundred years. Add, among other things, antibiotics, organ transplants, and oral contraceptives to the list of inventions and procedures that have both improved the quality and added to the complexity of our lives. Each innovation requires adaptation, and the more innovations, the more adaptations. Also, the more adaptations, the greater the potential for stress.

New machines, new methods, new materials, and new procedures are being introduced in an endless stream. Constant technological innovation requires an openness to learning and to starting new careers at midlife, which can be both challenging and stress-producing. Job stresses affect not only the parents but also the children and grandparents. When a father or mother loses a job and has to embark upon a new career, all members of the family have to respond to extraordinary demands for adaptation.

Job Stress

Consider, as an example, the stresses induced by the constant changes in computer technology. Within the past decade, the memories and speeds of computers have been vastly expanded. This means that the new machines can run more programs more quickly. This in turn means that those who work with computers must be constantly learning the new applications. To be sure, such changes keep computer operators on their toes, but they can also be enormously time-consuming and stressful. Since computer operators are also people with families, the effects of the rapidly changing technology will also be felt by their spouses and children.

Technological change and innovation can stress families in other ways. I met a cab driver recently who told me that he once owned his own uniform rental and dry cleaning business. The introduction of methods for permanently pressing fabrics and rendering them dirt- and oil-resistant did away with the need for his kind of professional dry cleaning. Today it is cheaper for companies to buy than to rent uniforms for their employees. The employees now have responsibility for the care of the uniforms. When the uniforms get soiled, the workers simply put them in their washing machines and dryers at home. With these new materials there is no need for the uniforms to be rented and professionally dry cleaned. As a result, society lost a dry cleaner and gained a cab driver.

Likewise, automation in factories has all but eliminated any number of time-honored professions such as lathe and drill press operators. Automated tellers in banks reduce the need for bank tellers, and so on. Every modern occupation is affected by technology. The physician or lawyer who has not brought a computer into the office for research, billing, and record keeping appears hopelessly old-fashioned and behind the times.

Craftspeople are as much affected by technology as the professionals. Plumbers and carpenters have to learn about new materials such as nylon pipes and pressure-treated woods if they are to remain competitive in their fields. In the same way, the seamstress must learn to operate the new computerized sewing machines.

Lifelong learning is the keynote in a technologically explosive society, an orientation at once challenging and stressful.

Separation Stress

The advent of jet travel in combination with the internationalization of industrial production has contributed to family stress in an important way. Because production is so scattered (for example, cars assembled in Detroit have components made in all parts of the world), travel has become an essential part of modern business. As international trade and production have grown, so has international travel. The introduction of the jet airplane has, of course, greatly facilitated the internationalization of business. I know many businessmen and business women who have to be away from home not merely days but weeks and months at a time. Separation from loved ones is stressful; it requires adapting to the absence of an important person in our lives.

Here again, grandparents may be called upon to fill in for an absent parent, and if and when they do, it may not be fully appreciated. Some parents returning from a long trip may wish to assume the parental role immediately, although children may not be ready as quickly to accept their authority. Grandparents can get caught in the middle and may even be blamed for the children's behavior. Parents need to be reminded that children, no less than adults, need time to make the transition from the grandparent to the parent frame of authority and nurturing.

✧ GENERATIONAL STRESS ✧

Rapid technological and social change can also produce generational stress. One way of looking at such stresses has been offered by famed anthropologist Margaret Mead. While her views are helpful in understanding the effect of social change on the relationships between generations, several of her conclusions have been misconstrued and have contributed to some of the contemporary problems between generations. Mead describes societies as being of three major types, or figures: postfigurative, cofigurative, and prefigurative.

Postfigurative Cultures

In postfigurative cultures, social structure, values, and behavior patterns are relatively fixed and permanent. The grandchildren learn the same information and learn it in the same manner as did their grandparents. In such cultures, older generations have considerable authority inasmuch as they have all the knowledge, values, and skills that are to be transmitted to the young. Parents and grandparents are thus experienced guides to their children and to their grandchildren. There is respect and deference for the older generation and effective cooperation between the generations.

Cofigurative Cultures

Cultures that experience a moderate rate of change are called cofigurative cultures. In such cultures the idea that the young will grow up in a somewhat different world from that of their parents is accepted. Parents are no longer the sole and accepted source of knowledge, values, and skills. Nor are they the only models for social behavior. In a changing society, teachers at school and the peer group within and outside it become increasingly important sources of authority. In our country, many children of immigrant families in the early decades of this century grew up in a cofigurative culture. Yet the parents still played an important role, as Mead wrote in 1970 (*Culture and Commitment,* New York: American Museum of Natural History, pp. 32–33):

> In . . . cofigurative cultures the elders are still dominant in the sense that they set the style and define the limits within which cofiguration is expressed in the behavior of the young. There are societies in which approbation by the elders is decisive for the acceptance of new behavior; that is, the young look not to their peers, but to their elders for final approval and change. But at the same time, where there is shared expectation that members of a generation will model their behavior on that of their contemporaries, especially their adolescent age mates, and that their behavior will differ from that of their parents and grandparents, each individual as he successfully embodies a new style, becomes to some extent a model for his generation.

In cofigurative cultures, young people lose some veneration for their cultural past and for their elders, and they place greater value upon and confidence in their peers than did the youth in the postfigurative cultures.

Prefigurative Cultures

When social change is extremely rapid, as it is in our society at the present time, Mead says the culture becomes prefigurative. In prefigurative cultures, the rapidity of social change is such that the young must spend the majority of their time adapting to what is new. There is little time if any to acquire the knowledge, skills, and values of the parents and grandparents in the postfigurative cultures. As a consequence, the younger generation loses much of its respect and veneration for parents and grandparents. There is an increasing alienation between the generations, since each has known a significantly different world.

In Mead's view contemporary parents and grandparents are still trying to raise children as if they were living in a postfigurative or cofigurative culture with many stable elements to be passed down from generation to generation. Young people, however, find it difficult to see much of value from the past in dealing with a future with so many unknowns and in a world so different from the ones their parents and grandparents knew.

Mead epitomizes the generational issue between cofigurative parents and prefigurative children in the following presumed dialogue (*Culture and Commitment,* p. 63):

> Cofigurative parents are wont to say, "You know, I have been young and you have never been old." Prefigurative youth are likely to respond, "You have never been young in the world I am young in and never can be."

The Prefigurative Child

Although Mead was writing from a cultural point of view, she has often been misread as speaking from a psychological or developmental point of view. Mead addressed the issue of changing cultures and values but has been read to be addressing the issue of children's adaptability to technology. According to this misinterpretation, prefigurative children are better adapted to the technological society than are adults. This in turn has led to a conception of enhanced child competence that has contributed to the contemporary hurrying of children to grow up too fast too soon.

To be sure, children are not awed by computers and microwave ovens in the way that their parents are. Children are not impressed by what they have grown up with, but this lack of respect should not be equated with adaptive competence. Children may take computers and microwaves for granted as part of the furnishings of their lives, but this does not mean that they understand them any better or are more proficient in their use than are their parents. In fact, just the opposite is true. Computers, for example, are to be found in every adult workplace from the supermarket to the service station. The one place computers have yet to be fully integrated is the public schools.

Development and Technology

The ease of contemporary youth with some facets of modern technology does not mean that they have skipped the stages of development to which all humans are subject. It is certainly true, for example, that I did not grow up in the world of sexual freedom and drug availability that my own children experienced when they were young. Nonetheless, I matured in much the same sequence of stages that they did. As an adolescent I was idealistic and rebellious, believed in my personal invulnerability, and was convinced that everyone was watching and thinking about me. We all go through the same stages of physical, emotional, and intellectual development regardless of the culture in which we mature, and we are all different because of the unique circumstances of our upbringing.

The erroneous extrapolation from Mead's writing that children in a prefigurative culture such as ours have everything to teach adults and nothing to learn from us is seductive. Parents are more likely than grandparents to fall into the prefigurative trap of assuming that children are the repositories of knowledge, values, and skills. For hurried, stressed parents, the image of the sophisticated, self-assured, independent child ready to take on whatever life has to offer is appealing. Children and youth may come to believe it as well. This places great stress upon young people because they really are not instant adults.

Children Are Less Adaptable Than Adults

The point of all this, and the one that we need to make with contemporary parents, is that children are the young of the species. They, like the young of all species, need adult guidance and direction. This is true regardless of whether the culture is postfigurative, cofigurative, or prefigurative. With respect to child rearing, biology takes precedence over culture.

It is easy to demonstrate this fact. When a family moves, for example, it is the children who suffer the most stress. The father and mother have, or can make, immediate acquaintances at work or in the neighborhood. Children, and particularly teenagers, may have much more trouble making new friends than their parents. Children flourish in the security and stability provided by the postfigurative cultures. Prefigurative cultures are most stressful on the young, not on the old. As the German novelist Herman Hesse wrote in the novel *Steppenwolf* (New York: Rinehart, 1963, p. 24):

> Every age, every culture, every custom and tradition has its own character, its own weaknesses and its own strength, its own beauties and ugliness; accepts certain sufferings as matters of course, puts up patiently with certain evils. Human life is reduced to real suffering, when two ages, two cultures and religions overlap. . . . Now there are times when a whole generation is caught in this way between two ages, two modes of life with the consequence that it loses all power to understand itself, and has no standard, no security, no simple acquiescence.

It is the young in the prefigurative culture who "lose their power to understand themselves, have no standard, security or simple acquiescence."

Thus, Hesse suggests that youth are less well rather than better adapted to a rapidly changing culture than are the adults. All the facts support this observation. On every measure we have, children and youth are doing less well today than they were a quarter of a century ago, when we entered the prefigurative period. Stomach aches and headaches at the preschool level; learning problems and depression at the school-age level; and substance abuse, crime, pregnancy, and suicide at the adolescent level have all shown marked increases over the last twenty-five years. During the same period, adult health has improved, and our longevity has increased. There is strong evidence that prefigurative cultures are more healthful for adults than they are for children and youth.

The Importance of Adult Attention

When the values, knowledge, and skills of a society are stable, they can be imparted by anyone, since they are common to everyone. In a prefigurative culture, however, parents and grandparents are the only ones who can teach the young certain values, standards, and beliefs. The young certainly will not acquire them in the schools or through the media. Nor are religious institutions an important force in shaping values and morals for a large portion of the population.

I have gone into this issue at length because it is so often misunderstood. Rapid social change and the pseudosophistication of our youth should not be an excuse for the abdication of parental and grandparental responsibility. Rather, these circumstances place even greater weight and importance upon us than when the culture is slower-paced. Yet when parents should be spending more time with their children, they are spending less. The effect of the resulting stress is reflected in the research results described above.

The Role of Grandparents

This need for adult attention places a great burden upon grandparents. Whether caring for their grandchildren for an extended time or for brief visits, grandparents often have to deal with children who are under stress. While grandparents should never undermine the authority of the parents, they should set firm rules and limits for their grandchildren when they are with them. If these are different from the parents' rules, grandparents can say, "These are our rules and our limits, and when you are with us, we expect that you will follow our rules. When you are with your parents, you have to live by their rules. We have our rules and they have theirs, and we are just different."

At a time of rapid social change, a clear-cut set of rules and limits is very important to children. They may resist them and rebel against them, and this is healthy too. Unhappiness is as much a part of life as happiness, and there is nothing wrong with children learning that important fact. It would be nice, and much easier for us, if we did not have to set limits and define values. But our role as grandparents in a prefigurative culture is also different than it was for our own grandparents living in a postfigurative culture. We are better adapted to making changes than are children. We may yearn for the kind of role our own grandparents played, but we have to play the role our own times have thrust upon us.

✧ MEDIA ✧

New roles are also required because of the vast changes that have occurred in the media. We generally think of media as providing information and entertainment. Yet information can be stressful. Hearing about an earthquake in an area where we have relatives can provoke anxiety. Entertainment can also be stressful. It is not just the horror films that can distress us; watching a football or basketball game can be stressful if we become overinvested in our team's winning or losing. The media can also stress us indirectly through images of ourselves and others. Let us look at some of the different media and how they stress families.

Television

When we think of television in connection with children, we often focus upon the frequency with which violence and sexual activity are presented. While these images certainly affect children, the images of particular categories of individuals affect them as well. How a particular group is portrayed in the media very much affects how the members of that group view themselves and how they are perceived by others. Some of the changing images of women, minorities, and grandparents are instructive.

Women and Minorities. In the last thirty years, there have been major changes in the ways women and minorities are portrayed. Women were once shown almost exclusively in domestic roles, and minorities were portrayed as the underclass. Most of that has changed now. Women and minorities are depicted in all occupations and socioeconomic classes. These changes in media images reflect both changes in society's perceptions of these groups and their actual social contributions.

Grandparents. Interestingly, the depiction of grandparents has also changed. When television was first introduced, almost no programs included grandparents. If grandparents were portrayed, the portraits were stereotypical. Usually the grandparents were retired and living in Florida or lived on a farm and were visited on Thanksgiving and Christmas. There was never a hint that grandparents might have an active sexual life or that they might entertain lively interests in the world beyond their families.

All that has changed now. TV shows like *Golden Girls* and *Empty Nest* make it clear that grandparents have many interests and active sexual lives. In shows like *The Equalizer* and *Falcon Crest*, actors and actresses of grandparent vintage are portrayed as strong and sexy. These images not only reflect changed images of grandparents in our society but also help grandparents see themselves in a different way. And other viewers, including grandchildren, record a different image of grandparents than they might have picked up twenty or thirty years ago.

This change in the television image of grandparents both reflects and contributes to the changed image of grandparents that has emerged in our society. Those of us with a bit of gray in the hair now can identify with leading men and women who reflect our good feelings about ourselves. Rocking chairs are out, and active, involved lives for grandparents are in.

Yet this new, more realistic portrayal of mature adults does have its downside. Grandchildren, for example, may take the TV grandparents as ideal models of grandparenting. They may compare their real grandparents with these TV ideals and find their own grandparents a little wanting. If a grandfather doesn't handle difficult situations with the ease and aplomb of the grandfather on the series *Our House,* the child may feel cheated. And grandparents may come to feel that they should behave like the TV models. Feeling that you have to live up to a screen image can be stressful.

It is helpful to watch such shows with our grandchildren and talk with them about the characters. Children are often quite perceptive of the reality of the portrayals, but they often do not realize their perceptions unless we take the time to draw them out. Then they often end up saying something like, "That's just made up." Such discussions often have fringe benefits. The problems depicted in the TV sitcoms can often be a springboard for the discussion of the real issues bothering our grandchildren.

Violence and Sex. A much more serious problem for parents and grandparents is raised by the prevalence of violence and sexually suggestive material on television. While this may be simply offensive to us as adults, it may have a more serious impact on our grandchildren. However, professionals disagree on the impact of televised violence and sexuality on children. Several conflicting theories have been suggested. One of these might be called the *instigation* theory. According to this view, children who watch violence and sexual activity are incited to engage in similar actions, although there is no clear-cut evidence that watching violence or sexual behavior instigates similar behavior.

There is also the *vicarious satisfaction* theory. According to this view, television violence and sexuality serve as a substitute for real action; children like violence because it gives them an opportunity to express frustration and anger without punishment and retaliation. In this regard it is interesting that both children and grandparents tend to enjoy professional wrestling. A great deal of aggression is expressed, but the consequences are innocuous. In this respect wrestling is much like the cartoons for children. What happens in those cartoons, as in wrestling, is that the victims of aggression get up immediately as if nothing happened to them. Such shows allow one to feel hostility and anger without guilt.

A third interpretation of the effects of television upon youth might be called the *inoculation* theory, which suggests that television renders children insensitive to violence and sexual activity. There is so much violence and sexuality on television that children become immune to them and no longer react to them in any meaningful way. The implication of this view is that this insensitivity acquired from television will render children impervious to the needs of others.

We have, unfortunately, no hard evidence to support any of these theories. Nonetheless, each one of them probably contains a bit of truth without being the whole story. Children who are inclined to violence may use something they saw on television as a starting point for their own aggression. But for such children, the starting point could just as easily have been something they read in a book or saw in a movie. In most television stories, the anger is usually resolved by the punishment of the guilty, the good guys winning over the bad guys. Other emotions are also fully resolved by the story, so there are no leftover feelings to be acted out in real life.

Nor is there any clear-cut evidence that children become insensitive to the human condition by the constant exposure to violence and suffering portrayed on TV. We have no data to the effect that children today are any less empathic toward their peers, pets, or strangers than were children in the past.

Effects of Television Viewing. Recent reviews of the literature on television give no support to the contention that television viewing reduces the amount of time children spend reading, lowers their grades, shortens their attention, or increases hyperactivity. Rather it is the messages children get via TV rather than the time spent watching television that seem to have the greatest impact upon them. The values that TV conveys and the images of different groups that it portrays are likely to have the most impact upon children and youth.

Films

Like television, films tend to reflect what is happening or has happened in our society. Yet films are less likely to affect our stereotypes and values than is television. This is true because many television programs come to us week after week. The characters become familiar, and we may mistake the actor for the character. When actor Ed Asner played newspaper editor Lou Grant on a television program of the same name, he was asked to address journalists at a convention! That was not likely to happen to Clark Gable as a result of his playing a newspaper editor in the movie *The Front Page.*

Common Themes. Films are most revealing about the stresses of the times when a number of them reflect a common theme. Apropos of our culture's being prefigurative, the current rash of so-called role reversal films is particularly instructive. In films such as *Back to the Future, Peggy Sue Got Married,* and *Eighteen Again,* a teenager, through one device or another, is suddenly empowered with the knowledge, wisdom, and judgment of an adult. Such film fantasies express the adult wish for children and youth to be better adapted to a rapidly changing society than adults themselves. This expectancy that children and youth display adultlike knowledge, sensitivity, and understanding is stressful to young people.

A twist on the reversal theme is presented in the film *Big.* In this film, unlike the others, the child is suddenly placed in an adult body. As an adult, the hero gets a job with a toy company and is enormously successful because of his practical yet creative approach to evaluating toys (essentially the approach of a discriminating child or young adolescent).

An interesting moment in the film occurs in a scene between the young man and his girlfriend, who also works for the toy firm. He is invariably playful, and his apartment is furnished with a variety of toys, including a trampoline. He finally gets the young woman to try it. She is reluctant because she is a hard-driving, no-nonsense career woman with no time for frivolous pursuits. However, she eventually joins him on the trampoline and ends up having a good time. Later she says to him that what draws her to him is that he is so "adult."

In an age when we expect infants to cope with separation and out-of-home care, when we expect young children to read and write before they enter kindergarten, and when we expect elementary school children to have a full program of extracurricular activities, this comment is very telling. There is no time for children to play in the prefigurative culture; it is all work so you can get into the right school, into the right college, and then into the right high-paying job. The only time you get to play is when you are an adult. The right to play is now something you earn as an adult after a childhood and adolescence of hard work.

This group of films, then, seems to reflect the attitude of many contemporary parents who believe that children should be our teachers and leaders. We have already talked about the fallacy of that proposition. Yet the fantasies on television and in the movies tend to reinforce it. That is why we have such a hard job counteracting it with our own children in discussions about our grandchildren. Television and films support parents in their belief that because children are better adapted to the society than adults, they can cope with everything and anything. The media thus reinforce an attitude that is very stressful to children and youth.

On the positive side, such films can be a starting point for talking about this whole issue. And it is well to point out that when the hero in *Big* has a chance to become a boy again rather than a successful young man with an attractive girlfriend, he chooses to return to his childhood. What helps him make his decision is watching children at play. He realizes then that he really does not want to skip his boyhood. Perhaps that scene is an omen that Hollywood, and it is to be hoped, TV, have at last recognized that you cannot skip stages in human development without paying a horrendous price.

✧ SCHOOLS ✧

Just as parents bring home the stress of work, children and teenagers bring home the stress of school. Of course not all young people are stressed by schooling any more than all adults are stressed by their jobs. But the rapid pace of social change has affected schooling, as it has all other facets of our society. Children and teenagers are stressed at school by excessive testing, overemphasis on homework, and often an intimidating social climate.

Testing

There is increasing pressure on the schools to be accountable for educating children and to enforce this accountability by achievement testing. Over the last decade, testing in schools has increased manyfold because it is assumed that academic achievement as measured by the tests is a clear way of demonstrating a school's effectiveness. As a result, the curricula in the schools are increasingly driven by the tests. The typical curriculum is now designed to prepare children for the tests rather than to ensure their grasp of basic concepts and knowledge. As the amount of testing has increased, so has the stress on children. Educators sometimes forget that taking a test is a stressful experience. The more tests, the more stress. Nor is the stress limited to the time of test taking alone. Children worry about the test in advance and about how well they did afterward.

As grandparents, we cannot cut down on the amount of testing done in the schools, but neither do we have to reinforce its negative impact. We have to restrain our tendency to ask how the child made out on this or that test and ask rather about what they know of this or that subject. If we emphasize knowledge in our discussions, we can communicate to our grandchildren that test scores are less important than what the child learned about the subject matter.

Homework

One of the biggest complaints many young people have is that they have too much homework. If as a grandparent you have charge of grandchildren while they are in school, this is an issue you will have to deal with. The most important rule is to act from knowledge rather than supposition. What is the homework assignment? What material has to be read? What problems have to be done? Knowing such things can give you a pretty good idea of how long it will take. If indeed it seems excessive, you can tell the child so, and suggest that the student raise the issue in class with the instructor. In many cases, however, the young person has exaggerated the extent of the homework. In at least some cases the homework could be done in the time the youngster spends complaining about doing it.

Other Stresses

The pressures and stresses children feel about homework and testing are real. In and of themselves they are not enough usually to harm the young person, but when these pressures are combined with other stresses, such as the absence of recess—time to relax from the academic grind—and a curriculum that may be inappropriate at worst and dull and unimaginative at best, they can add up to a child's feeling of being overwhelmed.

Junior high and high school students have to deal with bullying, theft, and sexual harassment. They must also deal with fellow students who cheat, who are on drugs, who drink at school, who become pregnant, and most sadly, who commit suicide. Many high schools now have students pass through metal detectors on entering school. All these experiences are stressful, and grandchildren bring the residues with them when they visit and show the effects when you visit them.

What Grandparents Can Do

We cannot change the schools, but we do not have to reinforce the pressures they place on children. Yes, tests are important and grades are important, but so are a child's emotional well-being and sense of personal worth. If our grandchildren are doing their best, we should support and reward them regardless of the grades they get. And we should not be reluctant to say that some of the homework is stupid if it is stupid. This does not mean we encourage young people to be disrespectful in school. It does mean that we should help them discriminate what is of value and what is not in educational materials. We should try, in every way we can, to soften the pressures of schooling. This means, at the very least, making it clear that grades are not the beginning and end all of human existence.

For grandchildren who are attending junior high and high school, we can listen to their stories of what goes on at the school. Sometimes we can suggest some strategies for handling particular situations that the teenager might not have thought of—like bringing along an older friend when the teenager expects a bully to make a move. And we need to talk with our grandchildren about drugs, suicide, and much more. These should not be lectures but discussions about real people and the problems and stresses that lead them into self-destructive behavior.

✧ RELIGIOUS INSTITUTIONS ✧

Churches and synagogues have always been the major social institution concerned with the welfare of families. In recent decades, however, there has been some estrangement between the family and the church or synagogue. For a variety of reasons, many religious institutions have lost the ability to deal effectively with the families they serve. Moreover, the rising divorce rate and the consequent appearance of single-parent families, blended families, and two-parent working families caught many religious organizations off guard. They were not fully prepared for dealing with these new family configurations.

Sometimes the position of a religious community is in conflict with what seems accepted in contemporary society. The Roman Catholic church's stand against contraception, for example, has placed some Roman Catholic couples in opposition to the positions of the religious hierarchy. In other congregations the ordination of female clergy has caused dissension. And among the more fundamentalist Christian denominations, the TV ministry scandals disillusioned many adherents and followers. To parents of all denominations, the one social institution they thought they could count on in time of need was not there for them.

The religious community is an important source of support for families and thus a buffer against stress. When the religious community does not support families, parents must look elsewhere. Many times they look to their own parents for support and guidance when before they might have sought out a minister, priest, or rabbi. While many grandparents may welcome and feel comfortable in this role, many others do not. Like it or not, it appears that the role of spiritual adviser is increasingly taken over by grandparents.

Fortunately, many churches and synagogues are moving back into support programs for families, and youth work is growing rapidly. Perhaps in response, families are beginning to return to their religious roots. In all denominations there are indications that membership and attendance at worship services is on the increase. This is a very positive trend. Research has demonstrated that one of the strongest bulwarks against many of the social stresses described in this chapter is a sense of community. And the religious community is the most accessible and hardiest community available to families. Joining a church or synagogue and becoming part of a religious community is one of the healthiest things families can do for themselves—parents, children, and grandparents.

These are some of the social pressures that stress families. When one member of a family is stressed—whether it is the parent at work or the child at school—the stress is transmitted to all family members. And when everyone in the family is being stressed at the same time, there is no one available with the emotional reserves to cushion the negative feelings and emotions of the other family members. Grandparents are often called upon at these times, and these demands for support stress them. Religious institutions can help relieve some of the family pressure.

CHAPTER 9

Healthy Coping and Caring

"When life hands you a lemon, make lemonade" is one of many time-honored homilies for dealing with stress. It suggests that stress is determined in part or wholly by the way we look at things. While it is certainly true that our attitude is very important in our assessment of and reaction to some types of stress, that is far from being the whole story. The homily, for example, certainly doesn't hold for the lemon life hands us at the death of a loved one. There is no way for a psychologically healthy person to "make lemonade" out of that. Sometimes the healthiest reaction we can have is sadness and depression or anger. Our attitude is more important for dealing with some types of stress than with others.

Stress in families comes in many different forms, and there is no single best way to deal with the seemingly limitless variety of stress situations. Nonetheless, it is possible to group types of stress and to describe some of the most effective ways of dealing with each type. In this way grandparents can have some effect on controlling stress without letting it control them.

✧ FOUR BASIC STRESS SITUATIONS ✧

Stressful events generally have two components: probability and control. Under the first component, some stresses, like getting hit on the head by a stone falling from a tall building, are highly unlikely. Others are highly probable. If we drink to excess, the probability of getting a violent hangover is exceedingly strong. The second component of many stress situations concerns the extent of our control over the event. For some stressful events, we can exert no control whatsoever. We really do not have any control over being rained out on graduation day. In other instances, such as drinking or eating to excess, we do have a great deal of control.

When we combine these two components of probability and control, we arrive at the four basic stress situations:

Type I. *Situations that are both foreseeable and avoidable.* For example, a grandmother recently asked me what to do about her two-year-old grandson, who always runs away from his mother when they visit a large shopping mall. No matter what the mother does in the way of threats and rewards, as soon as they are in the mall, the little one takes off. My suggestion was that they not take the boy to the mall! Of course, many Type I situations, such as getting a grandchild to avoid the predictable effects of drug abuse, are less easily resolved.

Type II: *Situations that are foreseeable but unavoidable.* It is easy to predict the effects of taking a grandchild to visit a seriously ill relative in a hospital. Yet we know that it is very important for us to make the visit and for our grandchild to be involved in the sad as well as the happy experiences of family life. Other Type II stress situations include activities such as going to a funeral, visiting a relative the grandchild dislikes but whom they must see for family reasons, and persuading them to take medicine they find distasteful. In each case avoiding the particular stress is likely to bring on even greater stress.

Type III: *Situations that are unforeseeable and unavoidable.* All disasters are Type III stresses. The sudden death of a loved one, an earthquake, or an automobile or airplane accident are neither foreseeable nor avoidable events. They are what in both legal and religious terms are referred to as acts of God.

Type IV: *Situations that are unforeseeable but avoidable.* This category seems, at first glance, to be rather nonsensical. If an event is unforeseeable, how can it possibly be avoidable? Nonetheless, when we give children a strong set of values, a solid sense of security, and self-esteem, we prepare them for whatever life has to offer, even if we can't predict what those offerings will be. We cannot predict, for example, what temptations a teenager will meet. Nonetheless, as a number of recent research studies have shown, if that young person has a strong set of values and beliefs, he or she has a sort of inner gyroscope that serves to guide them through the shoal-ridden passages of adolescence.

Religious faith is another way in which we prepare ourselves for the unpredictable but avoidable stresses in our lives. Of course, these preparations will not protect us from fatal accidents or natural disasters. Yet a set of strong moral and religious beliefs serves as an effective guide to decisions and conduct. Such beliefs provide inner cues and promptings that tell us to avoid involvements that could prove disastrous and they provide solace and comfort when we have to deal with the unavoidable and inevitable.

Let us look at each of these types of stress in a little more detail and at some of the ways we can most effectively cope with them and help our children and grandchildren cope with them. To do this, it is important first to identify the type of stress. If we can identify the type of stress we are dealing with, we can choose the appropriate strategy for dealing with it.

✧ IDENTIFYING THE TYPE OF STRESS ✧

To deal successfully with stress means that individuals and families have to learn to manage it. We do this by first identifying the type of stress situation we are confronting and then employing the strategy most appropriate for its effective resolution. Most of us have learned to do this in the course of growing up. We are, however, usually unaware of identifying a type of stress and choosing an appropriate strategy. But that is in effect what we do.

For example, if our baggage gets lost in transit and we are left at our hotel with nothing but the clothes on our backs for a week, this is stressful. Most of us take it philosophically and try to make lemonade out of the lemon. A philosophical outlook is the strategy of choice in such situations. Getting angry and depressed solves nothing and only adds to the discomfort we are already experiencing.

This, however, is not the strategy we employ when we deal with, say, a plumber or carpenter who has done a bad job or who appears to have overcharged us. For our own sake and as a model for our grandchildren when they are with us, we need to confront this person with our dissatisfaction. Such confrontations are stressful, but we hardly dare wax philosophical about them. Rather, we prepare for them by carefully rehearsing what we will say and how we will say it. One type of stress requires philosophy; the other, active planning and preparation. In most cases we recognize the difference without conscious reflection.

It is, nonetheless, helpful to identify this unconscious process of identifying the type of stress situation and strategy selection. In so doing, we gain much greater control over the situation, and control is the heart of successful stress management. A knowledge of the basic stress situations is also useful when we want to assist our children and grandchildren in dealing with stress. We can also help them identify the particular stress situations and choose the most useful coping strategies.

Accordingly, when we are confronted with a stressful situation that demands a response, the first thing to do is determine what type of stress we are facing. This will automatically clue us to the most effective coping strategy.

✧ TYPE I STRESSES ✧

Many events in our lives are both predictable and avoidable. Some of these arise with our own children, others with our grandchildren.

With Our Children

In earlier chapters we looked at some of the arrangements for caregiving expected of grandparents that might be a potential source of conflict and unpleasantness—in particular, the monetary arrangements. We can predict that unless these financial arrangements are made in advance, misunderstandings are likely to arise over who is to pay for what. This can lead to unhappy feelings all around. Accordingly, these stresses can be foreseen and avoided by making all of the money arrangements in advance.

This is sometimes much easier said than done. It is not easy to discuss financial issues with our children. We don't want to appear overly concerned about money, nor do we want to give our children the impression of miserliness. On the other hand, money is important. I have given it a lot of attention in this book because in my clinical experience it is one of the most frequent sources of family stress. Yet it is also the stress that we are the most reluctant to discuss openly and candidly.

The Symbolic Meaning of Money. In our society, and probably in most others, money is highly symbolic. Although the financial issues are important, even more important is what money symbolizes about our feelings for one another. In general, people handle money much as they handle their feelings. People who are outgoing and generous with their positive feelings are likely to be equally giving and generous with their money. Likewise, those people who do not easily give warmth and affection to others are likely to be correspondingly conservative with their money.

We all know this at some level, and we feel strongly that the way in which someone deals with us on a monetary basis reflects their feelings toward us as individuals. Even in the workplace, an unexpected raise is a symbolic expression of approval. In the same way, if our adult children are always thoughtful about our financial needs, as we once were of theirs, we appreciate the financial concern, but much more we appreciate what it says about their feelings toward us. Obviously, this symbolism of money and feelings works both ways. I emphasize dealing with the money matters up front because if we don't, we may be setting ourselves up for hurt feelings. And it is the hurt feelings, rather than a diminished pocketbook, that are the real stress to be avoided for the sake of the whole family.

We do have to discuss money matters even if we are fortunate enough to be in a position not to have to worry about money. This is true even if we have always been open and straightforward with our children about money matters as they were growing up. When our child marries, however, his or her mate may have different ideas about money, so we may have to start from scratch. Many times the money issue is really no problem, and our children are happy that we brought the subject up and that we got it resolved. Children of this kind would have been distressed if we felt badly and had not spoken out.

When There Are Disagreements. Children are not all alike, even children of the same parents. With some of our adult children and their mates, we can guess that this discussion of money may raise some hackles. With them, it is especially important to talk about finances. One way to begin is simply to say that it is better to talk about these matters in advance to avoid misunderstandings later. Then you can state what your impression of the financial obligations is and whether this is in agreement with their perception of the arrangement.

Suppose, however, there is a disagreement. Say the parents feel that you should be responsible for the groceries while you are caring for the grandchildren in their home while they are working or on vacation, and you feel that they should pay for them. This is unlikely, but it might happen. How do you go about resolving the difference? In all such instances, the basic strategy is to try to decide the issue on the basis of some rule or principle rather than on the basis of feelings and emotions. What might the rule be in this situation? A quite reasonable rule would be the following: "I am performing a service in looking after the children. I am not charging for that service, nor would I want to. But providing that service should not, in addition to my time, cost me money." Put more directly, one should not have to pay for the privilege of looking after one's grandchildren.

Stress Now versus Stress Later. At this point someone might well say that I am being contradictory. Earlier I wrote that it is important to confront a situation in advance to avoid conflict later. But isn't raising the subject of money itself a foreseeable and avoidable stressful event? If we don't raise the issue, we avoid a conflict. Am I not saying, then, that to avoid some foreseeable stress situations, we have to create others? Where is the net gain in stress reduction with this strategy?

Good question. Sometimes we do have to create a lesser stress in order to avoid a greater one later. Yes, raising the money issue is stressful, but it is a less intense and more manageable stress than one that might well arise if we did not have a preliminary discussion. Stress management does not mean avoiding stress entirely; it does mean bringing it under our own control.

Some readers may object that they are gentle people and that engaging in discussions about money is unseemly and opposed to their basic inclinations. Nonetheless, it is still important to deal with these money matters openly if for no other reason than to prevent our resentment from communicating itself to our innocent grandchildren and to safeguard our physical health. Our feelings, much more than our pocketbooks, are hurt by the thoughtlessness of our children. And hurt feelings that are not attended to can cause resentments that put our physical health at risk.

Recent research has shown that there is a link between personality types and heart disease and cancer. People who swallow their emotions and who cannot express their feelings when it is appropriate may predispose themselves to cancer. At the other extreme, individuals who are chronically angry and hostile can set themselves up for heart attacks and strokes. Body and mind are related. If we feel badly treated and are unable to put our feelings into words, we can make ourselves sick. What is healthy for our psyches turns out to be equally healthy for our bodies.

With Our Grandchildren

There are several Type I stresses that we can encounter with our grandchildren.

Substance Abuse. Suppose, for example, we suspect that a grandchild we are caring for is using drugs. We have talked this over with the parents, and they have the same suspicions. Here again we have the option of ignoring the situation, avoiding the confrontation, and hoping that it will go away by itself. Unfortunately, if left to themselves, such problems usually get worse rather than better. In most cases it is best to deal with the stress of confrontation now rather than the more serious stresses that inevitably accrue when such issues go unaddressed.

But what do we do? How do we confront a teenager with the issue of drugs? While there is no magic solution, some strategies work better than others. As grandparents, we can suggest the more effective strategies to our children and support and reinforce these strategies with our grandchildren. In this way we can present a strong and consistent generational position with respect to drug abuse.

First of all, it is important to realize that the teenager has a different perception of the situation than we do. Teenagers using drugs really believe that they are in control, even if they are not. In my many years of clinical work, I have found that if you argue with someone's reality, you only entrench that person more firmly in that reality. On the other hand, accepting the teenager's reality as our own doesn't work either. A young person would not really appreciate it if we said, "Oh, you have it under control. Great. I'm glad to hear it. Now I don't have to worry anymore."

In these circumstances I have found it best neither to argue with the teenager's reality nor to accept it. Rather, my approach is to recognize the teenager's reality as valid for him or her but not for me. I might say, "You may well be right, and you may indeed have this under control and can stop whenever you like. It doesn't seem that way to me, but I have been wrong before, and I can be again. Let's test it out. If you can stay drug-free for a week or a month, you will convince me. If you can't then we need to talk about getting you some help with the problem, okay?" This is a strategy we can suggest that our children use with our grandchildren and one that we will support and reinforce with similar statements. In this way we present a strong and consistent generational front.

Here we have challenged the teenager's reality in a very openly pragmatic rather than a closed, dogmatic way. By leaving the matter open, we direct the teenager to examine his or her behavior. If we simply attacked and said, "You are drug-dependent and I am putting you into a treatment program," the teenager's anger and resentment would prevent any self-examination. Rather, such a high-handed approach would arouse resentment and encourage the teenager to defend and justify his or her actions rather than examine them.

There is an important caveat in using the strategy of testing our different perceptions of reality. We have to mean it. Only when we communicate that we genuinely appreciate the teenager's viewpoint will our challenge to test out his or her control be accepted.

Foul Language and Disrespect. There are other foreseeable and avoidable stresses related to caring for grandchildren. If, for example, our grandchildren use bad language or show disrespect, we may feel inclined to wait for the appropriate moment to say something about it. Yet there will seldom be a better time than right now. Putting off the discussion just invites more of the same. Our natural tendency is to avoid the stress of an immediate confrontation in the hopes that the behavior will take care of itself and we won't have to say anything at a later time. Unfortunately, human nature doesn't work that way. If we don't say anything now, the bad language and disrespect are much more likely to get worse than better.

But what do we say? After all, what we call bad language and disrespect may not bother the parents. If we say something about it, aren't we in effect criticizing the parents? Isn't this to be avoided? Fortunately, there are other ways of handling such behaviors. We might say, for example, "I have to tell you that I don't really like to hear those words (or see you do that). If you wish to use that language (or act that way), please do it somewhere else, where I don't have to hear (or see) it." In this way we make our personal preferences known without saying that the words or behavior are absolutely bad. It is just that we disapprove of them. Again, it is much better for us, and for them, both psychologically and physically, to express ourselves in this way rather than to suffer in silence.

Other Type I Stresses

There are many other Type I stresses less serious than the ones we have just described. Many of these are best handled by keeping lists. A date list, for example, is useful to remind us to buy gifts for family birthdays and anniversaries. Remembering birthdays and anniversaries on time helps avoid unintentional hurt feelings and embarrassments. In addition to a date list, to-do lists are of great help in dealing with Type I stress situations. Such lists might help us, for example, remember to tell our teenage grandchild who is spending a vacation with us to keep a doctor's appointment.

In addition to date and to-do lists, we can make another kind that is also useful. This could be called a people list, on which we can annotate our list of birthdays and anniversaries.

These annotations can help us avoid certain very foreseeable stresses. To illustrate, next to a son-in-law's name, we might write, "Doesn't like my taste in ties, likes current best-sellers." Or we might note, "Moira is very sensitive about hair, avoid subject." By keeping a record of personal quirks, preferences, and aversions, we can remove or lessen the stress of many potentially hurtful personal encounters.

The Best Trait for Dealing with Type I Stresses

As the foregoing discussion suggests, the best trait we can develop for dealing with Type I stresses is *self-discipline*. Whether it be doing things now that we know need to be done eventually or saying things now that we would like to put off, the task is to deal with a certain amount of stress now to avoid a greater amount of stress later. The trick in life is not to avoid stress but to make it manageable, and we make it manageable by bringing it under our own control. This helps our children and our grandchildren directly, through the reduction or avoidance of stress on them and ourselves, and indirectly, through our modeling of appropriate and effective stress practices that they can follow themselves.

Over the years most of us have developed a number of self-discipline techniques that we can use to help us gird our loins to deal with Type I stresses. A time-honored technique for building self-discipline follows for those who do not already practice it: Do the most distasteful chore first and the most agreeable one last. In this way we have something to look forward to, a kind of treat for ourselves for having done the job we disliked doing.

✧ TYPE II STRESSES ✧

Type II stresses are those that are foreseeable yet unavoidable. Stress is really coincident with life, and therefore much of it is unavoidable. In fact, Type II stresses can encourage us to engage in productive activities. Knowing we have to discuss our grandson's low grades with his teacher can motivate us to talk things over with the boy in advance. The stress of having to prepare may encourage us to learn new communication skills and to polish old ones.

Visits from Grandchildren

There are, of course, many different Type II stresses and many different types of preparation. For example, if we know that we are going to spend some time with our grandchildren or that they are coming to spend some time with us, we are in a Type II situation. Even if we look forward to the visit, we also know that it means a disruption in our own schedules of eating, sleeping, and recreation. Our pleasant anticipation of the visit may be marred by its potential for interrupting our comfortable life pattern. This type of stress requires mental preparation. In dealing with an anticipated disruption of routine, we must focus on the positive. At such times we need to imagine the enjoyment we will have with our grandchildren: seeing their lively faces, hearing them call our names, and observing their remarkable growth. Preparing ourselves in that way is much more satisfying and much less stressful than fretting about how the visit will interrupt the comfortable routine of our lives.

Family Events

There are several other types of foreseeable but unavoidable stress situations that relate to our grandchildren. For example, there are some family events at which we know we are going to be uncomfortable. People whom we heartily dislike will be there, and we are going to have to be polite. Anticipating that event can be stressful. Here again, an effective mental strategy is to think about the positive aspects of the event. One strategy is to think of the people whom we will enjoy seeing rather than those whom we would prefer not to see. Sometimes it helps if we can find something humorous about the occasion. For example, the different types of people often brought together at a wedding can be funny. Imagine the liberal seated next to the bigot and the chic, sophisticated aunt forced to chat amicably with the ponytailed, earringed hippy nephew. These mental pictures take some of the unpleasantness out of the anticipation of and participation in a stressful but unavoidable social gathering.

If we feel comfortable at these events, we can help our grandchildren be more at ease as well. When we are not spending our time and energy avoiding certain people, we can use those resources to talk with our grandchildren. Moreover, our example of good humor and tolerance in the presence of unpleasant people is a useful and powerful one for our grandchildren to observe and copy.

Misfortunes

Other foreseeable but unavoidable stresses are the misfortunes of life. We will get sick at times, or things will not always work out the way we planned. Life can toss us a lemon at any time. This is true with respect to our grandchildren as well. Even when things are going well, we have to be careful not to become too self-satisfied or too complacent. This does not meant that we walk around with a constant sense of dread. But when we are feeling good, and when everything is going well, we need to enjoy it to the full because we can be sure it will not last.

The reverse, however, is also true. Just as the good times never last forever, neither do the bad ones. And when events have gone against us, we have to remember that it is both foreseeable and unavoidable that the good times will return again as well. What is positive about Type II stress situations is that both the pleasant and the unpleasant unavoidable events are bound to happen.

Coping with Type II Stresses

A useful motto for dealing with Type II stress is, Enjoy the good and prepare for the bad. Just as the key to coping with Type I stress is self-discipline, the key to coping with Type II stress is preparation.

Accidents, natural catastrophes, and unexpected deaths are all Type III stress situations, stresses that are neither foreseeable nor avoidable. Certainly the most stressful of all of these is the unexpected death of a loved one. Sometimes we have not only to deal with our own bereavement but with that of our grandchildren as well. How do you tell a child that his or her mother, father, grandfather, or grandmother died? Should the child be allowed to view the body, attend the funeral service, and go to the cemetery?

We need to look at these questions in a little more detail because they are some of the most frequent stress questions that arise for grandparents and grandchildren. First of all, my own opinion—and not all professionals agree with me—is that death should be dealt with when it happens and should not be part of a curriculum at school or a children's museum program. It is much more meaningful to talk about death with a child as a real event rather than as the subject matter in a book. We can, for example, discuss death when a pet dies or when we see a dead animal on the side of the road.

When a Child's Loved One Dies

First of all, it is important to remember that children do not understand the concept of death until they are about the age of eight or nine. Before that they think of death as a kind of going away. The second thing to remember is that although the child does not understand the concept of death, he or she does feel the loss of not seeing and being with the loved person. The child deeply experiences the loss even though he or she does not appreciate the reasons for it. Third, it is generally much better to talk about the person who is gone than to avoid talking about him or her.

The following case recently came to my attention: A ten-year-old girl and her seven-year-old brother were being looked after by their grandfather, whom they dearly loved. He had just made popcorn, and they were all sitting on the sofa together watching a TV program when he toppled over and died. With great presence of mind, the ten-year-old called her parents, who were at another couple's home for dinner. The children covered their grandfather and waited for the parents. When the parents arrived, they hugged their children and then quietly asked the children to tell them exactly what had happened.

The children attended the funeral, viewed the body, and went to the cemetery. Over the next weeks and months, the parents often encouraged the children to talk about their grandfather and about their feelings on the night of his death. The parents handled the situation in a way that was most healthful for the children and for themselves. The children were able to mourn their grandfather and then to get on with their lives.

Talking with Children about Death

When a loved one dies, how do we tell a child? Simply and directly and without metaphors. We should say something like "Grandpa died and we love him and will miss him very much." If a child below the age of eight or nine asks, "Why did Grandpa die?" it is always useful to ask the child what he or she thinks. Children often have their own ideas about such matters. Young children may even believe that it was something they did that caused the death. They may give up precious toys or not eat their favorite food as a way of atoning and trying to bring the loved one back. We need to reassure the child that he or she was very much loved and had nothing to do with Grandpa's death. We need say only that, "People die when they are old, and it is no one's fault. It is just the way it is."

If the children were present when the person died, as in the example, it is important to involve them in all parts of the funeral ceremonies as well. Children need to participate in the religious service and the burial to allow them to express their feelings and provide closure to what they have gone through.

When children are present at a death but not allowed to participate in the funeral service, they may feel that they were unjustly excluded. They feel, and quite rightly, that inasmuch as they were present at the death, they should be present at the funeral as well.

When the death of a loved one occurs at a distance, it is not necessary for the child to participate in the funeral events. In fact, for children below the age of six or seven, there is seldom any reason for the child to be present for the eulogy or the burial. Young children would not appreciate much of what is going on. It is important, however, to talk about the person who has died and to give the child an opportunity to talk about his or her memories and feelings. We need to do this deliberately and on a regular basis even if the children do not at first respond. They are listening and may need time to be able to express themselves.

Unforeseeable and Unavoidable Positive Events

Not all Type III stresses are negative. Some of the happiest and most enjoyable moments in life may be both unforeseeable and unavoidable. Psychologist Abraham Maslow wrote about what he called *peak experiences*. These are experiences of extraordinary pleasure, wonder, and awe that come upon us when we may least expect them—a glorious sunset that spreads its hues all across the sky, the mist in the morning that takes on an ethereal bluish hue and makes us feel we are in some enchanted place. Such experiences hit us with a rush and remain special moments in our lives. They are stressful and take adapting too, but what a joy!

Other positive Type III stresses include a surprise birthday or anniversary celebration. I know one couple who were celebrating their fiftieth wedding anniversary. They had expected to spend it quietly and then go off for a two-week cruise in the Caribbean. Their children and friends, however, had other plans. Under the guise of being taken out to dinner by their son and daughter-in-law, they were brought to a restaurant that had been reserved exclusively for the party. All their friends and family were there, including children and grandchildren from all parts of the country. What a pleasurable, unavoidable, and unforeseeable stress!

A General Strategy for Coping
with Type III Stresses

The most effective strategy for dealing with Type III stresses is a religious conviction, a philosophy of life, or a scientific credo. Whether our perspective is religious, philosophical, or scientific, it serves to get us out of ourselves. Negative Type III stresses push us to turn inward to see our personal misfortune as a greater tragedy than anyone else has ever experienced. At such times we may engage in that all too human tendency to feel sorry for ourselves. When these stresses are positive, on the other hand, they may tempt us to feelings of grandiose self-importance.

When we are dealing with a negative Type III stress, we need to remember that we are not the only one who is suffering; who has experienced injustice; or who feels lonely, neglected, and forgotten. Yes, we need to mourn, to feel sadness and loss, but we also need to get on with our lives. We help ourselves best if, after we have mourned over a death, we give ourselves over to the living. The best medicine for dealing with negative Type III stress is to help others. We see this in those parents or grandparents who lose a child to a drunk driver and then organize to strengthen the laws against drunk driving so that other young people will not die in the same way.

When we encounter positive Type III stresses, such as the anniversary party described above, we again see our good fortune in perspective. To be sure we are good people and have worked hard to attain what we have, and we have earned the love and affection that is now being shown us. Still we need to reflect that we had the good fortune to be born at a particular time and place and to have met someone who happened to be the right one for us and with whom we could share a long and rewarding life. While taking pleasure in this special occasion, and in our good fortune, we need eventually to get outside of ourselves once again.

A religion, a philosophy of life, a scientific credo are all ways of looking at life as a whole and our own place within it. We recognize that our pains and our pleasures are not unique and that we are, after all, only sadly, wonderfully, human.

✧ TYPE IV STRESSES ✧

Type IV stresses are unforeseeable but nonetheless avoidable. Yet how can this be? If something is unforeseeable, how can it be avoidable? It can because there are many stresses that we cannot foresee in any exact way but that we can foresee in a general way.

Temptation

Although we cannot foretell the particular temptations to which we will be subjected in life, we do know that we will be confronted with some type of temptation. We do not know what people or when some people will try to influence us to engage in behavior that runs counter to our moral and religious standards. But we can be sure that at one or another point in our lives we will have to deal with such influences. In today's world we can expect that from an early age our grandchildren will be confronted with numerous temptations and pressures to engage in unhealthy practices.

Strong Character as Preparation for Type IV Stresses

The best preparation for Type IV stress is a strong character. If we have deeply rooted values and moral and religious beliefs, we are less likely to be tempted than those who lack such well-planted convictions. That is why it is so important for grandparents to set a model of strong beliefs, standards, and values for their grandchildren. The role of grandparents is particularly important today, when children and their convictions have been challenged by all of the changes in social values and beliefs that have marked the last twenty

---

years. Our own children may not be the strong role models their children need.

When we demonstrate strong values and standards, young people can observe and gradually internalize them. In this way we can provide our grandchildren the inner strength they need to deal with the many unforeseeable but nonetheless inevitable temptations they will experience in the normal course of their lives.

Life is stress and stress is life, but we can make our lives and the lives of our children and grandchildren more rewarding and fulfilling if we learn to identify and manage the variety of stresses that are part of our human condition. Managing stress puts us in charge of our life and provides perhaps the most important ingredient for healthy, productive living, namely, hope. It is hope that enables us to continue when things are bad and not to become complacent when they are good. When we are able to manage our lives with self-discipline, preparation, philosophy or religion, and character, we discover that indeed, hope does "spring eternal."

INDEX

A

Absolutism, 56
Achievement-popularity conflict, 111
Activity overload, 114
Adjectives, 44
Adolescence
   definition of, 96
   development during, 10–11
   divorce and, 139–140
   eating disorders of, 118
   formal operations in, 100–103
   inconsistency in, 10–11
   intellectual development in, 99–103
   issues of, 110–118
   limit setting during, 112–115
   personal development in, 106–110
   physical development in, 97–99
   pregnancy during, 116–117
   quarrelsomeness in, 101–102
   school problems of, 110–112
   social development in, 103–106
   strategic interactions in, 104–105

Adolescence (*continued*)
   substance abuse during, 115–116
   world of, 10–11
Adolescence, 23
Adolescent crush, 102
Adolescents. *See* Adolescence
Adopted children, 94–95
Adults, opposition to, 76
Adventure stories, 106
Adverbs, 44
Advertising, to child market, 30
After-school work, 113–114
Age Wave, 130
Alcohol abuse, 115–116
Alcoholics Anonymous (AA), 116
Allegory, understanding of, 100
American frontier mentality, 25–26
American Indian tribes, attitudes in toward physical defects, 15
Animism, 56–57
Anniversaries, remembering, 170
Anorexia, 118
Aristotle, 18, 99

Asner, Ed, 155
Assumptive realities, 8
   dealing with changes in, 9–10
   lies and, 8–9
   testing of, 9
Athletic activities, 89–90
Attachment
   grandparent-parent, 126–127
   to grandparents, 123–126
   grandparent-to-grandparent,
      127–128
   to parents, 123
   as source of stress, 123
Austen, Jane, 13, 111
Authority, reverence for, 18
Automation, stress and, 144
Autonomy
   development of, 47–50
   will and, 49–50

B

Baby-sitting
   during childhood, 92–94
   ground-rules for, 93
Back to the Future, 155
Bed-wetting, 48
Behavioral modification, 20–21
Big, 155, 156
Birthdays, remembering, 170
Birthing, siblings present at, 37
Bladder control, 47–49
Blended families, 130–132
*Bodily Changes in Pain, Hunger, Fear
   and Rage*, 120
Body image, adolescent
   preoccupation with, 107
Bowel control, 47–49
Bridge Over Troubled Waters,
   116
Bulimia, 118

C

Cannon, Walter, 120
Causality
   growing understanding of, 57
   new sense of, 82
   understanding of during
      childhood, 81
Change, cultural adaptation to,
   145–151
Character, strength of, 178–179.
   See also Self-discipline
Child abuse
   motivation for, 4
   during preschool years, 73–74
Child care
   crisis in, 141–142
   out-of-home, 34–36
   during preschool years, 70–71
   quality of, 35–36, 50–51, 70–71,
      142
Child care services
   for preschool children, 70–71
   quality of, 35–36, 50–51, 70–71,
      142
Child-child relations, 13
Child development, 2
   in adolescence, 10–11
   in early childhood, 5–7
   in infancy, 2–5
   in middle childhood, 7–10
Childhood
   adopted children during, 94–95
   baby-sitting during, 92–94
   definition of, 75–76
   development in, 7–10
   early, 5–7
   effects of divorce in, 137–139
   extracurricular activities
      during, 80–81
   grandparent's role in, 87–88
   intellectual development
      during, 81–84
   lesson taking during, 89–92

Childhood (*continued*)
  personal development during, 84–88
  physical and mental development during, 76–80
  special issues of, 88–95
  television viewing during, 92
  world of, 1–11
Child-parent relationship. *See* Parent-child relationship
Childproofing, importance of, 42
Child psychology, 23–24
Child rearing
  changes in over past two decades, 27–32
  and changing laws regarding children, 30–31
  cultural influences on practices of, 14–17
  divorce and, 27–28
  in drug culture, 29
  in dual-career couples, 27
  faddish practices in, 37
  fathers' increasing role in, 31–32
  history of practices in, 12–32, 18–27
  implications of intellectual development in, 82–83
  less support for, 29–30
  nature tradition of, 21–25
    resistance to, 25–27
  need for new learning materials for, 28–29
  nurture tradition of, 19–21
  scientific knowledge about, 19–27
  sociocultural focus in, 18–19
  technology and, 28
  in urban versus rural communities, 28
Children
  cognitive development of, 24–25

Children (*continued*)
  effects of divorce on, 136–140
  need for adult attention in, 150
  need for guidance of, 148–151
  in opposition to adults, 76
  prefigurative, 147–148
  rights of, 31
  as teachers and leaders, 148, 155–156
Child Study Movement, 23
China
  ancient, 15
  sociocultural focus in, 19
Chinese Americans, low juvenile delinquency rate in, 16–17
Chores, during preschool years, 55
Church. *See also* Religious faith
  as central authority, 18
  pressures of, 159–160
Citizenship, 18
Civilizations and its Discontents, 24
Classifications, elementary, 62
Cognitive conceit, 9
Coincidental causality, 57
Color discrimination, 34
Communication, during first year of life, 40–41. *See also* Language development
Computers, stress and, 143–144
Concrete operations, 100
Configurative cultures, 145–146
Conflict, resolution of, 68–69
Coordination
  good, 78
  lack of, 77–78
Culture(s)
  adaptation to change in, 145–151
  child-rearing practices and, 14–17
  heterogeneous, 16–17
  homogeneous, 14–16
Curfews, 113
Curiosity, emergence of, 44

D

E

Exclusivity, 103–104
Exploration, support for, 54–55
Extracurricular activities
  during childhood, 80–81
  choice of, 89–90
  overload of, 114
  parent-grandparent
    disagreements over, 91–92
  when child wants to stop,
    90–91

F

Fairy tales, 61
Falcon Crest, 152
Family, 119
  blended, 130–132
  divorce and changing patterns
    of, 128–140
  dual-career. *See* Dual-career
    family
  single-parent, 119, 133–136
  sources of stress in, 122–123
    from events of, 172–173
    relationships as, 123–128
  stress Type I in, 165–171
  two-parent working, 141–142
Fantasy, 61
Fathers
  increased role of in child
    rearing, 31–32
  role of in care of newborn,
    36–38
Fears, healthy, 67, 73–74
Fiction, read during childhood, 81
Fight or flight reaction, 120–121
Films
  social change reflected in,
    155–156
  themes of, 155–156
Financial stresses, 165–166
Foot binding, 15

Foreign language
  learning in first year, 45–47
  motivation to learn, 46
  spoken by grandparents, 46
Formal operations, 100
  interactions with parents and,
    101–102
  peer relations and, 102–103
  schooling and, 100–101
Frames, 64–65
  clashes of, 65
  spoiled, 66
  switches in, 64–65
Freiburg, Selma, 53
French, Marilyn, 126
French culture, individualism and
    group pride in, 15–16
Freud, Sigmund
  on dependency needs, 5
  nature tradition and, 23–24
Froebel, Friedrich Wilhelm
    August, 22

G

Games, with rules, 77
Generational stress, 145
  adaptability and, 148–150
  adult attention and, 150
  in configurative cultures, 145–
    146
  development and technology
    in, 148
  grandparents' role in, 150–151
  in postfigurative cultures, 145
  prefigurative child and, 147–
    148
  in prefigurative cultures, 146–
    147
Generativity, 125
Golden Girls, 152
Grandchildren, visits from, 172
Grandmother-mother conflict, 126

Infancy (*continued*)

second year of (*continued*)

intellectual development during, 43–44

language development during, 44–47

physical development during, 42–43

social development during, 50

Infants. *See also* Infancy; Newborn

divorce and, 136–137

intelligence of, 3

motor maturity of, 2–3

self-knowledge from observation of, 4–5

temperament of, 3–4

Information processing, in preschool age children, 58

Initiate, development of, 55

Intellectual development

during adolescence, 99–103

during childhood, 81–84

in early infancy, 39–40

grandparent's role in, 83–84

implications of for child rearing, 82–83

in second year, 43–44

Intelligence

clues to, 1–2

physical development and, 2–3

school performance and, 7–8

Intermarriage, child rearing and, 17

J

Japan, family pride in, 15

Jobs

for adolescents, 113–114

stress of, 143–144

Journal of Genetic Psychology, founding of, 23

K

Keller, Helen, 79

Kindergarten, origin of, 22

King Lear, 13

Knowledge, growth of during preschool years, 61–63

L

Language. *See also* Language development

characteristic mistakes in, 59–60

facility for in young children, 1

foreign, 45–47

foul, 169–170

gaining fluency in, 62 ·

helping child learn, 45

Language development

in preschool age, 58–61

in second year, 44–47

Laws

protecting children, 30–31

protecting children's rights, 31

Learning, through play, 69–70

Lessons, 89–90

disagreements between parents and grandparents over, 91–92

when child wants to stop taking, 90–91

Lies, assumptive realities and, 8–9

Limit setting

activity overload and, 114

on after-school work, 113–114

curfews in, 113

for grandchildren living in grandparents' home, 135–136

grandparents' role in, 114–115

on peer group activities, 112–113

P

Parent-child relationship
  in Bible, 13
  constants in, 12–14
  literary theme of, 13
  television and, 71–72
Parents
  attachment to, 123
  divorce and remarriage of,
      129–130
  formal operations and
      interactions with, 101–102
  need to assert self with child,
      49–50
  personality of and infant
      temperament, 3–4
  travel of and separation stress,
      144–145
Parker, Dorothy, 111
Peak experiences, 176–177
Peers
  formal operations and relations
      with, 102–103
  limits on, 112–113
  teenage pregnancy and
      pressure of, 117
Peggy Sue Got Married, 155
Permissiveness, 22
Personal development
  during adolescence, 106–110
  during childhood, 84–88
  grandparents' role in, 87–88
  moral behavior and, 85–86
  sex differences in, 86–87
Personal fable, 108–109
Personal identity
  failure in formation of, 109–110
  sense of, 106–107
Personality
  stress reaction and, 121
  type, link of to heart disease
      and cancer, 168
Pestalozzi, Johann Heinrich, 22
Peter Pan, 76

Physical development
  during adolescence, 97–99
  during childhood, 76–80
  in children with special needs,
      79–80
  coordination and, 77–78
  in early infancy, 38
  early or late, 98–99
  in second year of life, 42–43
  sex differences in, 97
Physical handicaps, 79–80
Piaget Jean
  on adolescents' reasoning, 100
  on intellectual development, 39
  nature tradition and, 24–25
  resistance to in United States,
      26
Play
  cooperative, 63
  lack of in prefigurative culture,
      156
  during preschool years, 69–70
Playing frame, 64–65
Popularity-achievement conflict,
      111
Porter, Cole, 29
Positive events, stress of, 176–177
Postfigurative cultures, 145
Prefigurative cultures, 146–147
  child in, 147–149
  elimination of play in, 156
Pregnancy, teenage, 116–117
Premarital sex, teenage
      pregnancy and, 117
Preschool years, 53–54
  child abuse during, 73–74
  dangers to child during, 73–74
  differences in thinking
      patterns during, 56–58
  discipline during, 67–69
  effects of divorce in, 137
  information processing during,
      58
  knowledge and learning
      during, 61–63

Q

R

S

School (*continued*)
  problems with during
      adolescence, 110–112
  reasons for poor performances
      in, 111–112
  stresses of, 156–159
  violence and crime in, 158
Science
  as authority, 18
  theories of on child rearing,
      18–27
Second Changes, 136
Second year, 41
  autonomy in, 47–50
  intellectual development in,
      43–44
  language development in,
      44–47
  physical development in, 42–43
  social development in, 50
Security objects, 57
Self-assertion, 49
Self-conception, development of, 85
Self-consciousness, 107–108
Self-definition, 107
Self-discipline
  in coping with Type I stresses,
      171
  in coping with Type IV
      stresses, 178–179
  importance of in child rearing,
      20
Self-reliance, 76
Selye, Hans, 122
Sensory discriminations, in early
      infancy, 34
Separation stress, 144–145
Seventh-grade slump, 110–111
Sexuality, in children, 23
Sexual repression, 24
Shakespeare, 13
Sharing, unwillingness for, 2
Shopping frame, 65
Siblings
  fighting between, 68–69

Siblings (*continued*)
  rivlary between, 13
      formal operations and, 102
Similes, understanding of, 100–101
Single-parent families
  and coping with child
      returned to nest, 134–135
  coping with grandchildren of,
      135–136
  stress of, 133–136
Skinner, B.F., 20–21
Slow-to-warm-up child, 3
Social change, stress and, 120
Social development
  during adolescence, 103–106
  in second year, 50
Social interactions, in teenagers'
      literature, 105–106
Socialization
  frames in, 64, 65–66
  manners and, 66
  during preschool years, 63–66
Social status, exclusivity and,
      103–104
Social stress, 141
  and generational stress, 145–
      151
  media and, 151–156
  religious institutions and,
      159–160
  school and, 156–159
  technology and, 142–145
  and two-parent working
      families, 141–142
Sociocultural focus, 18–19
Soviet Union, sociocultural focus
      in, 19
Space, conception of, 81
Special needs, 79–80
Speech, development of,
      44–45. *See also* Language
      development
Sports teams, 89–90
Stagnation versus generativity,
      125

Thoughts Regarding Education, 19–20
Time
  conception of, 81
  measurement of, 82
Toilet training, 47–49
  lapses from, 54–55
Tom Sawyer, 82
Travel, separation stress and,
    144–145
Trust, development of in first
    year, 41

U

United States
  environmental tradition in, 20–21
  heterogeneous culture in, 16–17
  individualism in, 15
  nature tradition in, 22–23
    resistance to, 25–27
Urban communities, 28

V

VCRs, 73
Verbal precociousness, 1

Verbs, 44
  errors in tenses of, 59–60
Viewpoint, inability to see
    another's, 6, 57–58
Violence on TV
  innoculation theory of, 154
  instigation theory of, 153
  vicarious satisfaction theory of,
    153–154
Visual memory, in early
    childhood, 6

W

Waiting in line frame, 64
Walking, 42
  versus talking, 44
Wallerstein, Judith, 136–139
Watson, John, 20
Willfulness, 49–50
Winnie the Pooh, 81
Words, first, 44. *See also* Language
    development
Wylie, Robert Ross, 130

ABOUT THE AUTHOR

David Elkind is Professor of Child Study at the Lincoln Filene Center at Tufts University, MA, and author of numerous books on child and adolescent development. Among his best known books are *The Hurried Child: Growing up Too Fast, Too Soon; Miseducation: Preschoolers at Risk;* and *All Grown up and No Place to Go: Teenagers in Crisis.* He writes also for national and international publications, scholarly and popular, and is on the editorial board for *Parents* magazine as well as for several professional journals. A past president of the National Association for the Education of Young Children, Dr. Elkind has become known for his outspoken efforts to help teachers and parents provide a supportive environment for youngsters to reach their full growth potential in their own appropriate developmental time.